GIOVANNI PICO della MIRANDOLA

Commentary on a Poem of Platonic Love

Translated by

Douglas Carmichael

Professor of Philosophy
St. Lawrence University

UNIVERSITY
PRESS OF
AMERICA

LANHAM • NEW YORK • LONDON

Copyright © 1986 by

University Press of America,® Inc.

4720 Boston Way
Lanham, MD 20706

3 Henrietta Street
London WC2E 8LU England

Library of Congress Cataloging in Publication Data

Pico della Mirandola, Giovanni, 1463-1494.
   Commentary on a poem of platonic love.

   Commentary on Benivieni's poem Amor dalle cui.
   Translation of: De hominis dignitate, written in
Italian.   The Italian text used for this translation
is from the 1942 ed. of De hominis dignitate, edited
by E. Garin.
   Bibliography: p.
   Includes index.
   1. Benivieni, Girolamo, 1453-1542. Amor dalle cui.
2. Love in literature.   I. Carmichael, Douglas,
1923-   .   II. Benivieni, Girolamo, 1453-1542.   Amor
dalle cui.   1986.   III. Title.
PQ4610.B4A83613   1986   851'.3   86-1606
ISBN 0-8191-5259-5 (alk. paper)
ISBN 0-8191-5260-9 (pbk. : alk. paper)

All University Press of America books are produced on acid-free
paper which exceeds the minimum standards set by the National
Historical Publications and Records Commission.

TO MY WIFE, EMMIE

ACKNOWLEDGMENTS

The text of the present translation is based on that established by Professor Eugenio Garin his Giovanni Pico della Mirandola, De Hominis Dignitate, Heptaplus, De Ente et Uno. Firenze, Valleci Editore, 1942. In the notes to this volume I have availed myself whenever possible of the source identifications in Professor Garin's edition. I have been assisted in the publication of this work by a Faculty Grant from St. Lawrence University. For the identification of some of the biblical references I am indebted to Professor Daniel W. O'Connor of the St. Lawrence Department of Religious Studies and Classical Languages, and for help on some of Pico's more puzzling passages I owe a great deal to Professor Henry W. Garrity of the St. Lawrence Department of Modern Languages and Literatures. For putting the book into its present format my thanks are due to Mrs. Jean F. Deese, secretary to the St. Lawrence Department of Philosophy.

TABLE OF CONTENTS

INTRODUCTION

However it may be defined, love plays a major role in human existence. In spite of this fact, few major philosophers have had much to say about it since Plato wrote the <u>Symposium</u> and the <u>Phaedrus</u>. In recent years, however, there has been a growing philosophical interest in what love is, how its principal sub-types resemble, differ from, and otherwise relate to one another, and what function any and all of them play in the dynamics of the universe. An increasing number of colleges and universities offer courses in the philosophy of love. A Society for the Philosophy of Love and Sex holds annual meetings in conjunction with the American Philosophical Association. There are even occasional books on love being published by philosophers with recognized academic credentials.[1]

One philosopher of earlier times who did write on love was that meteoric figure of the Italian Renaissance, Giovanni Pico della Mirandola. Every so often in human history there appears a figure who seems to embody the ideals of an age or culture, to exemplify to a surprising degree what his contemporaries most envy and admire. Such a person was Sir Philip Sidney in Elizabethan England, and another such was Pico della Mirandola in Renaissance Florence. His friend Angelo Poliziano wrote of him "Nature seemed to have showered on this man, or hero, all her gifts. He was tall and finely moulded; from his face a something of divinity shone forth. Acute, and gifted with a prodigious memory, in his studies he was indefatigable, in his style perspicuous and eloquent. You could not say whether his talents or his moral qualities conferred on him the greater lustre. Familiar with all branches of philosophy, and the master of many languages, he stood high above the reach of praise."[2]

The handsome and wealthy younger son of a princely house, a lover and a poet, a scholar and linguist of unusual precocity who amazed all by his erudition, an intimate of Florence's Medici potentate Lorenzo the Magnificent, Pico flashed briefly but brilliantly across the sky of the learned

ix

world before turning to the religious intensities of
Savonarola and dying at thirty-one. Born in 1463 to
one of the families of petty despots who ruled the
cities of northern Italy, Pico apparently became
disgusted with his elder brothers' squabbling over
their joint inheritance and decided early to devote
himself to scholarship. At the universities of
Bologna, Ferrara, Padua, Pavia, and Paris, he
studied, first, canon law, then literature and the
scholastic philosophy of the Middle Ages. At the
same time he learned Greek and became familiar with
the thought of Plato, Aristotle, and the various neo-
Platonists. He also learned Hebrew, Arabic, and
Aramaic, then known as Chaldean, and employed other
scholars in these languages to make translations for
him. On an early visit to Florence he became a
friend of Marsilio Ficino and Angelo Poliziano and a
leading member of their informal neo-Platonic
Academy.

In 1486 Pico conceived the idea of drawing up a
number of theses, or propositions, to express the
beliefs for which he felt ready to offer an
intellectual defense. On his way to Rome to set this
project in motion, he stopped off at Arezzo, which he
left in the company -- probably voluntary -- of a
married woman. Pursued by the outraged husband,
some of Pico's men were killed, and he himself was
wounded and captured. The affair was smoothed over
through the intervention of Lorenzo, but it seems to
have given Pico a more serious outlook on life. He
had already burned his youthful love poems, and now
he devoted himself in earnest to the formulation of
his theses.

There were nine hundred of them, and he felt
some difficulty in keeping the figure this low. They
were drawn from a great variety of sources, but more
than half seem to have originated with Pico himself.
He published them in Rome and at all the universities
of Italy, challenging all comers to debate them
against him. In a gesture worthy of his princely
rank, he offered to pay their travel expenses to Rome
for the purpose.

The great debate never came off. It was
prohibited by the papal authorities, who found
thirteen of Pico's theses heretical. He got himself
into deeper trouble with a so-called Apology and was
able to make his peace only with a later pope, again
thanks in large measure to the influence of Lorenzo.
Meanwhile Pico had settled in Florence, largely
retired from public disputes though continuing his
study and writing. Though maintaining his friendship
with the other Platonists of the Medicean circle, he
came increasingly under the influence of Savonarola
and died in an atmosphere of austere sanctity in
1494.

Of his major works, the best known is probably
his Oration on the Dignity of Man, which was intended
as a sort of general introduction to his theses for
the abortive debate. The essay Of Being and Unity
was to be part of a never-completed project for the
reconciliation of Plato and Aristotle. His longest
completed work, the Heptaplus, is an interpretation
of the account of the creation in the first chapter
of Genesis on seven different levels of allegory.

The Commentary on a Poem of Platonic Love was
most probably written in 1486,[3] though some scholars
date it as late as 1491[4]. It contains many references
to the approaching debate on Pico's theses. During
Pico's lifetime it circulated widely in manuscript,
but it was not published until 1519, well after his
death, and even then only in a collection of the
works of the poet being commented on, Girolamo
Benivieni. Pico had met Benivieni on his first visit
to Florence in 1479 and exchanged Latin love poems
with him. Benivieni's Poem of Platonic Love offered
Pico a platform from which to attack some of the
ideas expressed in Ficino's commentary on Plato's
Symposium, and his commentary on the poem was meant
to serve as a preface to his own projected, and
presumably better, commentary on the Symposium, as
well as foreshadowing some of ideas of the Heptaplus.
Professor Eugenio Garin, argues that the 1519
version, published by Biagio Buonacorsi, seems to
have been modified to give less offence to Ficino,
who was a relative of Buonacorsi and whose
interpretations of Plato are frequently criticized
more strongly in the surviving manuscript versions.

Benivieni was a leading member of the circle of Florentine Platonists and wished to compose a definitive poem on love to rival those of Guido Cavalcanti and Guido Guinizelli, with the first of whom Pico compares him in some detail. He had shown his poem to Pico by November of 1486, and Pico soon conceived the idea of using it as the basis for his own treatise on love, even if it was some time before he fully completed it. The close relationship between the two men is shown by the encomium on Benivieni in one of Pico's few surviving poems.

The Commentary is Pico's only major work in the vernacular rather than Latin, and its vocabulary shows that he was accustomed to thinking in Latin, frequently using words that never passed over into Italian. Its sentences are long and complicated, often equivalent to modern English paragraphs, and I have frequently taken the liberty of breaking them where Pico uses semi-colons.

It is strictly only in virtue of its title that Pico's work is a commentary on Benivieni's poem at all. In reality it is an essay on love in three books, although he follows them with an almost line-by-line interpretation of the poem showing how his own ideas are there figuratively presented. These ideas, in turn, are based mainly on Plato's Symposium, with some reference to other dialogues, particularly the Phaedrus and Timaeus, as interpreted by Plotinus and various lesser neo-Platonists. Some minor adjustments are made for Christian orthodoxy, but rather than attempting fully to baptize Plato, Pico takes refuge in the exact wording of Benivieni's title, A Poem on Love Composed . . . According to the Thought and Belief of the Platonists. Benivieni in his preface to the Commentary states that Pico and he had long withheld the publication of their related works from concern over Plato's compatibility with Christian doctrine, and Benivieni affirms his own Christian intent in the publication. It was an age when the Inquisition was active. Pico himself, however, does not take any special pains to dissociate himself from any doctrines on which Plato's orthodoxy could be challenged.

The Commentary's first book is devoted to
setting forth the metaphysical background necessary
for the ensuing discussion of love. Pico adopts
Plotinus' trinity of the One, the Divine Intellect,
and the World-Soul, presenting them as God, the
Angelic Mind, and the Rational Soul, with individual
rational souls apparently taken as aspects or
subdivisions of the latter.   (For this reason I have
sometimes translated the phrase with capital letters
and sometimes with lower case.) He distinguishes
three modes of being -- causal, formal, and
participated -- as well as making the more familiar
distinction between form and matter, and he also
distinguishes three levels of created creatures --
corporeal, intellectual, and mixed.   The terms
intellect and reason are not synonymous but refer to
different levels of cognition.   The Platonic Ideas
have their causal being in God, their formal being
in the Angelic Mind, and their participated being as
concepts in the Rational Soul.

The second book is concerned with the definition
of love and beauty. Echoing Dante and St. Thomas,
Pico defines desire, or love in the broadest sense,
as an inclination towards whatever is or seems good.
In a more narrow sense it is the desire to possess
and enjoy the beautiful, though God cannot love in
this sense since in His perfection He cannot lack or
desire anything. The natural object of desire is
the end towards which each thing naturally tends,
the perfection by which it participates in the divine
goodness and attains the highest degree of happiness
of which it is capable. The ultimate common object
of all natural desires is God.   Some desires,
however, are not natural but based on knowledge, and
since the knowledge is fallible these may go astray
from the good. Yet every desire must already possess
its object if only to the extent of knowing what it
wants.

If love is the desire for beauty, it cannot be
fully understood unless beauty is defined also.
Beauty, like love, has both broad and narrow senses.
In a broad sense, beauty is the combination of two or
more parts in a harmonious whole. In a narrow

sense, it is a property peculiar to visible objects.
There are, however, two sorts of visible objects
corresponding to the two kinds of sight, corporeal
and intellectual, the latter being best described as
the intuitive cognition of patterns and relations.
To the two kinds of sight there correspond two
beauties and two loves, the heavenly and the vulgar.
The highest beauty is that of the Platonic Ideas,
combined by God with formless matter in the creation
of the Angelic Mind. Since the Ideas have lost their
perfection by separation from their source and
mixture with matter, the Angelic Mind wishes to
attain them in their full perfection, and this love
turns it towards God, a movement similar to the neo-
Platonic concept of epistrophe.

This turning to the higher is also
characteristic of all the nobler loves Pico describes
in Book III. The true heavenly love is the love of
the Angelic Mind for the Ideas in their causal being
in God. What Pico calls "the image of heavenly love"
is that of the Rational Soul for their formal being
in the Mind. This is the highest form of human love.
Below it is the vulgar appetite for the visible
beauty of shapes and colors. This vulgar love also
has its divisions. Human love in a second sense, the
more common, is the love of sensible beauty separated
by imagination as much as possible from the body.
Lowest of all comes the bestial love focused on
bodily union.

Within every man, however, there remains a
vestige of the angelic love for the higher beauty. If
souls can break away from excessive concern for their
bodies, they may rise again towards ideal beauty.

Following these three books of general
introduction, Pico offers a detailed stanza-by-stanza
analysis of Benivieni's poem, showing how it
illustrates the general points he has been making.
Some points already made get still further developed,
such as the idea that physical beauty depends not
only on the nature and arrangement of parts but also
on the infusion of grace, which is beauty in the
proper sense and must come from the soul, but the
principal item of philosophical interest here is

Pico's exposition of Benivieni's version of the ladder of love in the _Symposium_. Like Plato's ladder, it has six steps plus a suggestion of a seventh, and some of the steps are perhaps ascended by stages.

Plato's lover starts with a love for one beautiful body and goes from that to a love for all beautiful bodies, to that for souls, for laws and customs, for branches of knowledge, to a single science of beauty and finally to the vision of absolute beauty itself. Pico's ladder starts like Plato's with the love of one beautiful form. On the second step, however, the lover refashions the physical image in his imagination, making it more spiritual and perfect. On the third, the soul abstracts the universal beauty from this particular sensory image. These three steps are all levels of vulgar love. On the fourth step the soul becomes aware of the power of abstraction it has just employed and finds in itself the image of ideal beauty, for which it feels "the image of heavenly love". On the fifth step the soul rises to an intellectual approach to ideal beauty, for which its own particular intellect, however, is inadequate. On the sixth, therefore, it merges with the Angelic Mind and achieves a complete awareness. The seventh step, unattainable except by the love with which God loves Himself, would be a final reunion with God. Presumably only God can be fully united with Himself.

For Plato the ladder of love is essentially of concern only to particular individuals seeking eternal possession of the highest beauty. For Pico, however, the importance of the ladder is not so much personal as metaphysical. The highest love that most mortals may hope to attain is only an image of the intellectual desire for intellectual beauty, the heavenly love felt by the Angelic Mind for God. As rational, each human soul may participate in the Rational Soul's love for the Mind, but this is only an incomplete imitation. Love is a part of the circular movement whereby each angelic or rational nature attempts to return to its source, there to find its highest felicity.

In his exaltation of the heavenly love, Pico perhaps becomes an even more ardent advocate of "Platonic" love than Plato himself. From what we know of his life, however, it becomes apparent that he at least thought he had experienced all the steps of the ladder that man could climb and that he had at least an idea of what might still lie beyond his reach.

[1] E.g. Solomon, Robert, Love: Emotion, Myth, and Metaphor, New York, Doubleday, 1981, and Van de Wate, Dwight Jr., Romantic Love, A Philosophical Inquiry, University Park, Pennsylvania State University Press, 1981.

[2] Quoted in Symonds, John Addington, Renaissance Italy, London, Smith & Elder, 1877, p. 329.

[3] Garin, Eugenio, ed., Giovanni Pico della Mirandola, De Hominis Dignitate, Heptaplus, De Ente et Uno, Firenze, Vallechi, 1942.

[4] Vignal, L. Gautier, Pic de la Mirandole, Paris, Grasset, 1937.

COMMENTARY OF THE ILLUSTRIOUS LORD
COUNT GIOVANNI PICO DELLA MIRANDOLA
ON A POEM ON LOVE
COMPOSED BY GIROLAMO BENIVIENI
A CITIZEN OF FLORENCE
ACCORDING TO THE THOUGHT AND BELIEF
OF THE PLATONISTS

BLASIUS BONACURSIUS TO GIROLAMO BENIVIENI,
HIS DEAR FRIEND, GREETINGS

All the scholars of our times, my dearest
Girolamo, as well as those of the future, ought
surely to mourn continually the premature death of
the admirable young Giovanni Pico, Prince of
Mirandola, since because of his outstanding virtues
they have suffered so great a loss of the advantages
which they could promise themselves from his life, a
loss suffered not only by those interested in
philosophical and Platonic studies but also by all
lovers of holy scripture. The former he has already
much gratified with excellent works which have not
yet been made public, and he seeks here to gratify
the latter by demonstrating the great utility and
glory of the Christian religion. This gratification
is balanced by his unexpected and lamentable death,
but I believe that scholars and men of letters will
endure it patiently, considering that Almighty God
does nothing without great mystery. I believe it is
divine providence that has now put it into the minds
of our printers to make public by their art this
prince's elegant and erudite commentary on your
learned and graceful poem on divine love according to
the thought and belief of the Platonists, in order
that it may not remain neglected and forgotten and
that not only his friends but all men of letters may
have opportunity to enjoy it, plucking thence the
fruit which they cannot harvest from his other works
not yet brought to light.

Having in my hands a manuscript of this poem and
commentary and being begged for it with great
insistence by some of our printers, I have been
somewhat doubtful whether I ought to release it to
them or not. On the one hand I have been restrained
by the knowledge of how repugnant, for reasons
understood by you, the publication of such a work
would be to your mind and the author's. On the other
hand, I have been moved by the urging of the
printers, by the wishes of many, and by the
advantages and convenience in which it seemed to me
such publication would result.

Conquered ultimately by the exhortations and
prayers of my friends, I chose to have this
manuscript of mine copied by the afore-mentioned
printers with some consideration for you, even though

2

against your will, since to retain it would defeat
the wishes of many, and I thought that my fault would
be as much more excusable as a private offense is
less than a public one, since the latter, beyond the
common good, has as its goal the personal welfare of
a friend. Having word of other manuscripts of this
work which are being read in various places and
circulated by many hands, I thought it impossible
that it should not one day be published in the same
fashion, which would be much less acceptable to you
and all friends of the Count, since such manuscripts
would be imperfect and full of many errors of which I
believe my own copy has been, if not completely, at
least for the most part purged. And if in all this
you still find me at fault, excuse me to yourself and
to the happy memory of the author of this commentary
for the love which recognizes neither restraint nor
law, so that all those who read it will be able, if
my judgment does not deceive me, to recognize easily
that if the Count had also had the opportunity to
write of love in a Christian fashion, as was his
intention, he would have done so with such felicity
that the truly divine teaching would have surpassed
and excelled that of Plato and all the other
philosophers. Farewell.

GIROLAMO BENIVIENI, A CITIZEN OF FLORENCE, TO THE READER

Giovanni Pico, Prince of Mirandola, a man truly admirable in all respects, reading, as happens among friends, a poem of mine in which, inspired by a most enjoyable reading of our friend Marsilio Ficino's erudite commentary on Plato's <u>Symposium</u>,[1] I had squeezed into a few verses what Marsilio most elegantly describes in many pages, took pleasure in discussing it in a commentary no less learned and elegant than copious, motivated, I believe, not so much by the merits of the thing as by the tender and singular affection which beyond all credibility he always showed towards me and my works. In looking at this poem and commentary again later on, however, lacking some of that spirit and fervor which led me to compose it and him to interpret it, there was born in our minds a shadow of doubt as to whether it was fitting for any who profess the law of Christ and wish to talk about love, especially heavenly and divine love, to discuss it as Platonists and not as Christians, and we thought it would be well to suspend the publication of such a work at least until we saw whether, through any revision, it could be transformed from a Platonic work into a Christian one.

Soon after this deliberation there followed the premature and, more than any other calamity of these times, unfortunate and lamentable death of that Giovanni Pico, at the unexpected occurrence of which, almost out of my senses and full of confusion and revulsion at all worldly things, I thought of leaving this poem and commentary, as well as many of my other verses, to the judgment of dust and burying them away for ever. Although I have observed this course of action until now, the eager desire of others has nevertheless been more able to bring this work to light than my scruples and diligence have been to withhold it. The original manuscript having already come into the possession of certain curious people along with other books and commentaries by this Giovanni Pico, perhaps through the indulgence and permission of those who had them, they were given into the hands of the printers and used by them

almost before I had notice of it. Not being able
honestly to prevent this, and on the other hand not
seeing in the publication of such a work any fault of
my own, I thought, as I have said, that I should let
it go ahead out of natural courtesy. Placing great
trust in the prudence, kindness, and orthodoxy of
those who persuaded me to do this, I now pray that
whoever reads it should be able, in all places where
in following the teaching of Plato this poem or
commentary departs in any way from Christian truth --
going beyond the irrefragible reasons adduced to the
contrary by our theologians, especially by the most
angelic doctor St. Thomas Aquinas -- to accept the
authority of Christ and his saints rather than the
opinion of a gentile. Let him excuse our errors, if
they can indeed be called errors, in presenting
simply and without any approval the opinion of others
even if not true, excusing it, I say, with the
superscription or true title prefixed to this poem
and commentary, by which it is clearly stated that we
wished to treat of love not according to the Catholic
faith but according to the thought and belief of the
Platonists.

In the execution of this task, if there are
still any errors besides those already mentioned, and
there may well be many others, this merit and
advantage cannot be taken away from it, that Platonic
scholars reading attentively may find in this
commentary many insights by means of which the eye of
their intention can more easily and perhaps with
another perspective penetrate to the inmost marrow of
some of the more remote meanings of so great a
philosopher.

[1]Commentary on Plato's Symposium, tr. S. R.
Jaynes, Columbia, University of Missouri, 1944.

A POEM OF LOVE
COMPOSED BY GIROLAMO BENIVIENI,
A CITIZEN OF FLORENCE,
ACCORDING TO THE THOUGHT AND BELIEF
OF THE PLATONISTS

Stanza I

Within his hands Love holds the reins that
  guide
My heart, and in his sanctified domain
That flame does not disdain
To feed, which there he kindled to a blaze.
Love puts my tongue and talent under strain
To utter what my bosom holds inside.
My heart is terrified
At such a task; my tongue lacks proper phrase.
That which is in me struggles in a maze,
And yet my thoughts of love must be expressed;
Against a greater force, no force prevails.
And Love has pledged my feeble art, for sails,
Those wings on which he first approached my
  breast,
Embellishing its crest,
For ever leaving there those glorious plumes
Whose living light illumes
My heart and gives me hope to show revealed
Those mysteries which now he keeps concealed.

Stanza II

I tell how Love from fountainhead divine
Of uncreated good descends down here,
When born, and whence the sphere
He moves, and shapes all souls, and rules the
 world,
How then in human hearts he'll disappear,
With what proficient arms of what design
He'll make the human line
To heaven lift its face from earth uncurled,
How blazing up he burns, in flamelets swirled,
To heaven why this one he steers, to earth
Another turns, a third lets rest between.
My weary rhymes and verse of languid mien,
Who now on earth to pray for you has worth?
A yoke too snug of girth
Bears down our necks to make Apollo yield
To prayers our hearts can wield.
Come, Love, your promised feathers I invite
To guide my feeble wings on sightless flight.

Stanza III

Reflected from the one true heaven, celestial
 light
Into the great Angelic Mind descends,
Its firstling, which it tends
And nourishes beneath the living leaves.
Innate desire this universal Mind now bends
To crave and seek its primal blessing's height,
And makes the power ignite
Which in its breast rich patterns interweaves.
From this that first desire its task achieves,
Miraculously kindles, changing Mind
To uncreated radiance's Sun.
That heat, that flame, that burning never done,
Which, from the darkling Mind and light
 declined
From heaven mingled, shined
In the Angelic Mind, is love's own fire,
First born, devout desire,
From poverty and wealth, when Heaven made
The one to whom in Cyprus awe is paid.

Stanza IV

Because the lovely Cyprian's fair breast
Sustained that god when first he saw the light,
It roused his appetite
To track her living beauty's blazing sun.
Therefore our first desire, to expedite,
He bound with new-made hemp and firm behest
To follow him in quest
Of goods, until we reach the foremost one.
For whom by Love what lives in him's begun,
In him by Love the fire is lit, and lo --
His heart, in dying, burns and, burning, grows.
For him the deathless fountain overflows,
With that which moves the heavens down below;
That light which makes us go
Aloft, by him directed, showers down.
On us, his works to crown,
That living Sun bestows such aureoles
That everlasting love inflames our souls.

Stanza V

As from the Highest Good eternal Mind
Has being, lives, moves, understand, portrays,
The Soul unfolds, displays
For it what shines upon its godly breast,
And what that bosom squeezes tight it sprays
Abroad. Then what to live and move's designed,
With Soul superbly twined,
Is moved and lives and feels and does its best.
As down from Heaven to Intellect progressed,
From Soul down here is Venus born, whose grace
Lights up the sky, roams earth, and clouds the
 world.
Reflected in the Sun, its light half-furled,
The first is wont to contemplate her face.
As all her beauty's base
Lies in the radiance It sheds on her,
So her light she'll confer
Upon the last. As heavenly Love has sat
With this, just so the vulgar follows that.

Stanza VI

When first formed by the face of God, the Soul
Departs in order to descend down here,
From that exalted sphere
Where dwells the Sun, to enter into human
 hearts.
There manifesting with amazing arts
That worth she brought from stars that rule her
 role
And which, compacted whole,
Remains among her spoils from heaven's marts,
In human seed, as best she bears its smarts,
She makes her lodging, but of form and stamp
Repugnant more or less to heavenly care.
Whenever from the Sun that's graven there
An imprint on some seemly soul lays clamp,
Then blazes up its lamp.
The soul which bears it brightens with its rays
And feigns, the more to praise,
The mark more fair, and thus, despite its
 creeds,
The loving heart on sweet delusion feeds.

Stanza VII

The heart on sweet delusion feeds, and views
Its cherished inner image as its child,
To be sometimes re-styled
Beneath the holy light's resplendent streams,
A rare and heavenly gift, and hence by mild
Ascent from step to step the heart pursues
That birthless Sun, whose hues
Will tint the cherished image, beckoning
 dreams.
One Sun from three refulgent mirrors gleams,
Rekindling with its visage every grace
Which spirit, mind, or body beautifies.
From here the showy spoils are seized by eyes.
The other handmaid who there has her place
Takes them from eyes to trace
New traits, not shown. The many varied charms
Of sense the heart disarms,
To form a concept where what nature's done
In all is pictured in a single one.

9

Stanza VIII

Thus Love with this delights the soul and
  heart.
On this it dotes as on a first-born boy,
And views the truth with joy,
Though seen but as a sunbeam under waves.
Some flashes from the god must help decoy
The tender heart from darkness to depart
And higher beauty chart,
Which, from the peak of lower, one still
  craves.
Not just a shadow there its vision laves,
Which credence in the First Good gives us here,
But light, true likeness of the one true Sun.
Thus, once the heart the lustrous trail's
  begun,
Within its mind that glory will appear.
To light more sharp and clear
Thenceforth it flies, suspended near that orb,
Its brilliance to absorb,
By which in love are formed and beautified
The mind, the soul, the world, and what's
  allied.

Final Stanza

My song, I feel Love gathering up the reins
As daring boldness gives my heart the spur,
Perhaps beyond its best-appointed course.
Rein in desire, pull back the bit with force,
Turn virgin ears when vulgar love makes stir.
If higher love confer
On anyone its figure and its dress,
Love such a one will bless
Not with its leaves alone but with its fruit.
The rest have those, of this are destitute.

BOOK ONE

Chapter One

<u>That every created thing has its being in three</u>
<u>modes: causal, formal, and participated.</u>

The Platonists hold as their principal dogma
that every created thing has its being in three
modes, which, although they may be differently named
by different writers, nevertheless in one sense are
agreed on by all and may now be called by us causal
being, formal being, and participated being. This
distinction cannot be expressed in more familiar
terms but may be made clearer by an example. In the
sun, according to philosophers, there is no heat,
because heat is an elemental quality rather than a
heavenly one. Nevertheless the sun is the cause and
source of all heat. Fire is hot and is hot by its
nature and by its proper form. A log of wood is not
hot by itself but can easily be heated by fire,
participating through it in the aforesaid quality.
Therefore this thing called heat has causal being in
the sun, formal being in fire, and participated being
in the log of wood or other such material.

Of these three modes of being the noblest and
most perfect is causal being, and therefore the
Platonists would have every perfection which
is held to be in God to be in Him in this mode of
being, and for this reason they say that God is not a
thing but the cause of all things, likewise that God
is not intellect but is the source and principle of
all intellect.

These statements give great trouble to modern
Platonists from their basis' not being understood.
I remember that a distinguished Platonist once told
me that he was much astonished at a statement by
Plotinus, where he says that God understands nothing
and knows nothing.[1] It is perhaps even more to be
wondered at that this man did not understand the way
in which Plotinus means that God does not understand,
which is simply than that this perfection of
understanding is in God in the mode of causal being

11

and not that of formal being. This is not to deny the understanding of God but to attribute it to Him in a more perfect and excellent mode. This being so, one can now understand that Dionysius the Areopagite, the prince of Christian theologians, who holds that God knows not only Himself but also every least particular thing, is using the same mode of speech as Plotinus when he says that God is not of an intellectual or intelligent nature but indescribably exalted above all intellect and knowledge.

Therefore this distinction is to be carefully noted, because we shall often make use of it and it furnishes great light for the understanding of Platonic theories.

[1]Enneads V,vii, 40.

Chapter Two

That all creatures are divided into three grades.

The Platonists divide all creatures into three grades, of which two are extremes. In one are included all corporeal and visible creatures, such as the heavens, the elements, the plants, the animals, and everything composed of the elements. In the other are understood to be all invisible creatures, those not only incorporeal but also free and separate from everything bodily, those which are properly said to be of intellectual nature, and by theologians to be of angelic nature.

Between these two extremes there is a nature which, although it is incorporeal and invisible and immortal, is nevertheless the mover of bodies and assigned to this service. This is called the Rational Soul, which is subordinate to the angelic nature and placed in authority over the corporeal, subject to the former and mistress of the latter. Above these three grades is God, the creator and beginner of all creatures, which have their causal being in the divinity as their original source, and proceeding from Him immediately into the Angelic nature have their second kind of being, formal.

12

Ultimately, in the Rational Soul, He shines by means
of the Angelic nature in which it participates.
Therefore the Platonists say that divinity is
composed of three natures: God, the Angelic Mind, and
the Rational Soul, beneath which no being can claim
the term _divine_ except by abuse.

Of these three natures it would be possible to
make more explicit description and articulate
division, dividing bodies into different sorts, and
also souls, and telling which ones are called
animals, and which ones animated but not animals, and
why the world is called an animated animal by Plato
in the _Timaeus_.[1] But this discussion we shall keep
for its proper place, and here that by itself is
enough which is necessary for understanding the
treatment of love.

[1]30b.

Chapter Three

How the Platonists prove that God cannot
multiply
Himself but is the sole principle and cause of
every other divine thing.

Of these three natures -- God, the Angelic
Mind, and the Rational Soul -- the Platonists and the
Peripatetics and our own theologians show by very
obvious reasons, which it would be superfluous to
recite here, that the first, God, cannot be
multiplied but is a single God and the principle and
cause of every other divine thing. On the second
nature, the angelic and intellectual, there is
disagreement among the Platonists. Some, like
Proclus, Hermias[1], Syrianus[2], and many others, place
between God and the World-Soul, which is the first
rational soul, a great number of creatures, some of
which they call intelligible and some intellectual,
and even Plato sometimes confuses these terms, as
when he speaks of the soul in the _Phaedo_.[3] Plotinus,
Porphyry, and most of the more thorough-going
Platonists place between God and the World-Soul only
one creature, which they call the Son of God, because
it was directly produced by God.

The first view is more in conformity with
Dionysius the Areopagite and the Christian
theologians, who suppose an almost infinite number of
angels. The second is more philosophical and more
in conformity with Aristotle and Plato and followed
by all the Peripatetics and better Platonists.
Therefore, having proposed to speak of what we
believe to be the common opinion of Plato and
Aristotle, we shall leave aside the first view,
although it alone is true in itself, and follow the
second.

[1]Alexandrian Neo-Platonist of late 5th century,
a disciple of Proclus.
[2]Alexandrian Neo-Platonist of early 5th century,
teacher of Proclus.
[3]79c-e.

Chapter Four

That God produced from eternity a single incorporeal and intellectual creature, as perfect as it could be.

Following, therefore, the opinion of Plotinus,
which is accepted not only by the better Platonists
but also by Aristotle and by the Arabs, especially
Avicenna, I say that God, from eternity, produced a
creature of incorporeal and intellectual nature as
perfect as it is possible for a created thing to be.
On this account, He produced nothing else, because
from a most perfect cause there can proceed only a
most perfect effect, and what is most perfect cannot
be more than one as, for instance, the most perfect
of all colors cannot be more than one, because if
there were two or more, one of them would necessarily
be either more or less perfect than the other.
Otherwise one would be the same as the other, and
thus they would not be many, but one. Therefore that
which is less perfect than the other will not be most
perfect.   Likewise, if God had produced another
creature beyond this Mind it would not have been most
perfect, because it would have been less perfect than
that.

14

This is the reasoning which I am accustomed to adduce in support of this opinion, and it seems to me more effective than that which Avicenna uses, which is based on the principle that from one cause, in so far as it is one, there cannot proceed more than one effect.

But since these matters are introduced here only for a better understanding of what is principally proposed, there is no need to waste time on a more exhaustive examination of them. It is enough to know this: that according to the Platonists no other creature comes from God immediately but this first Mind. I say "immediately" because God is also said to be the cause of every effect which both this Mind and every other cause afterwards produce, but only the mediated and remote cause.

Therefore I am surprised at Marsilio, who holds that according to Plato our souls are immediately produced by God, which is not less repugnant to the school of Proclus than to that of Porphyry.

Chapter Five

By the Platonists and by the ancient philosophers Hermes Trismegistus and Zoroaster this first creation is called now Son of God, now Wisdom, now Mind, and now Divine Reason, which they also interpret as Word. Let everyone take careful heed not to think that this is what is called the Son of God by our own theologians, because we understand by the Son the same essence as the Father, equal to Him in everything, ultimate creator and not creature. What the Platonists call Son of God ought to be compared rather to the first and highest angel created by God.

Chapter Six

Of two modes of being, Ideal and Formal.

For the statement of what follows, it should be
known that every cause which by skill or intellect
works some effect has first in itself the form of
what it is about to produce, as an architect has in
himself and in his mind the plan of the edifice which
he wishes to build, and looking at that as a model he
constructs and produces his work in imitation of it.
Such a form as this the Platonists call an Idea or
archetype, and they hold that the form of the
building which the builder has in his mind has truer
and more perfect being than the actual building then
produced by him in a suitable material, whether stone
or wood or other such things. This first being they
call ideal or intelligible being. The other they
call material or sensible being, and so if a builder
builds a house they will say that there are two
houses, one intelligible, which the builder has in
his mind, and the other sensible, which is
constructed by him of marble or stones or whatever,
explaining that the Form can be in the matter only to
the extent that he has conceived it within himself.
This is what our poet Dante touches on in a poem
where he says "Whoso would paint, who cannot be the
picture, cannot draw it."

The Platonists say therefore that although God
produced only a single creature, nevertheless He
produced everything, because in that Mind He produced
the Ideas and Forms of all things. There is,
therefore, in that Mind the Idea of the sun, the Idea
of the moon, of men, of all the animals, of the
plants, of the stones, of the elements, and in
general of all things. The Idea of the sun being a
truer sun than the sensible one, and so on, it
follows not only that God has produced all things but
also that He has produced them with the truest and
most perfect being that they can have, that is, ideal
and intelligible being. For this reason they call
this Mind the intelligible world.

Chapter Seven

How this world was from eternity caused and produced by that first Mind, and how it is animated by a most perfect Soul above all other souls.

They hold that this mind caused the sensible world, which is an image and copy of the intelligible one. Since that is the archetype, the most perfect of all created things, in imitation of which this world is made, it follows that even this world is also as perfect as its nature allows. Therefore, because every animate thing is more perfect than the inanimate, and those which have rational and intelligent souls are more perfect than those animated by irrational ones, it is necessary to grant that the world is animated by a Soul more perfect than all others.

This is the first rational soul, which, although it is incorporeal and immaterial, nevertheless is bound to this function of moving and ruling corporeal nature. On this account this Soul is not as free and separate from its body as is that Mind by which it was produced from eternity, just as that Mind was by God. From this is drawn a very clear argument that according to Plato the world cannot be other than eternal, as all the Platonists also agree, because this soul being the eternal Soul of the world and not being able to be that without a body, as they will have it, this worldly body must also exist from eternity, and thus also the motion of the heavens, because the Soul, according to the Platonists, cannot exist and not move.

I have said that all the Platonists agree that the world is eternal because both Atticus[1] and Plutarch[2] and others who hold this present order of the world to have had a beginning do not on that account hold that before this there was nothing but God, as our Catholic church puts it, but believe that before this orderly motion of the heavens and present arrangement of earthly things there was a disorderly and turbulent motion governed by a depraved and sickly Soul. Thus they would allow infinite worlds

17

to have existed because the world has been reduced to
order from the confusion of chaos an infinite number
of times, and infinite times it has been returned to
that. With this the opinion of the Talmudists seems
to agree, who asked what God was doing from eternity
and answered that He was creating worlds and then
laying them waste, although following the basic
principles of the cabalists we can give their words
both a truer and a more fitting sense. Aristotle
attributes this opinion to Plato and on that account
sometimes says of him that he alone begins time
again, and sometimes, as in Book XII of the
Metaphysics, confesses that according to Plato motion
has been eternal.[3]

[1]Probably the 2nd century philosopher, a few of
whose fragments are preserved by Eusebius.
[2]Cf. Platonic Questions II, 2.
[3]Chapter vi, 1071b 32, in reference to Timaeus
30a.

Chapter Eight

How the three above-mentioned natures, God, the
    Angelic Mind, and the Rational Soul, are
signified by the three names Uranus, Jupiter[1],
and Saturn, and what is meant by them.

These three primal natures, God, the first Mind,
and the World-Soul, are by the ancient theologians,
who concealed their mysteries under poetic veils,
denoted by the three names Uranus, Saturn, and
Jupiter. Uranus is the god who produces the first
Mind, called Saturn, and by Saturn is generated
Jupiter, who is the soul of the world. Because these
names are sometimes confused, so that the first is
called Jupiter, and the World-Soul Saturn, and the
Mind Jupiter also, we shall give the basis and reason
for these names, comprehending which we shall
understand that all those variations and mutations
which seem made gratuitously and at whim proceed
harmoniously from a single principle.

I say, therefore, that this name <u>Uranus</u> signifies everything foremost and excellent above all other things, just as the first heaven, the firmament, is super-eminent above all corporeal things. <u>Saturn</u> signifies the intellectual nature, which alone is capable of understanding and contemplation. <u>Jupiter</u> signifies the active life which consists of ruling, administering, and moving by its command the things subordinate and inferior to it. According to the astrologers these two properties are found in the planets signified by the same names, Saturn and Jupiter, because, they say, Saturn makes men contemplative and Jupiter gives them principalities, governance, and the administration of peoples. Because the contemplative life is concerned with things higher than the one who contemplates and the active life with those lower, which are ruled and governed by what is superior to them, every nature, in so far as in some way it turns towards things lower than itself, involves itself in the active life.

Assuming this explanation of these names, we shall have to consider their propriety for these three natures, and it will be clear which name is suited to each of them and why.

[1]Pico refers to these gods as Celius and Jove, but I have substituted the names <u>Uranus</u> and <u>Jupiter</u> as more familiar, especially in the astrological references to the latter. The deities appear to be the same.

19

Chapter Nine

Of the variation of the three names Uranus, Saturn, and Jupiter, and why and how they suit the three above-mentioned natures.

As to the first, God, one cannot understand Him as contemplating because this is the property of the intellectual nature, of which God is the cause and source. He cannot be called Saturn because He alone is understood to be the beginning of all things. In this understanding are included two things. The first is His super-eminence and excellence, which every cause has over its effect, and for this reason He is called Uranus. The second is the production of that which proceeds from Him, in which is understood giving attention to lower things while He is producing them, which we said above to be like the active life. For this reason the name Jupiter is in some ways suitable to him, especially with the addition of the highest perfection, as in the name Jupiter Optimus Maximus.

To the first Angelic Mind more names are suited because it is less simple than God and more diversity is seen in it. First it should be known that every creature is composed of two natures. One of these is called potentiality, or the lower nature, the other actuality, the higher nature. Plato in the Philebus calls the first the unlimited and the second the limit or end.[1] By Avicebron[2] and others they are called matter and form. Although among the philosophers there may be difference of opinion as to whether this unformed nature is the same in all creatures, or whether it is different in natures of different grades, nevertheless all agree on this: that everything which lies between God and prime matter is a blend of actuality and potentiality, and this is enough for us. It does not matter for our purpose in what way this mixture or composition may exist or be understood.

Likewise, therefore, the first Mind is composed of two parts, and every imperfection in it is there in respect to the part called potentiality, and every perfection in respect to the other. In this Mind three operations can be considered: one in regard to the things superior to it, another in regard to itself, and the third in regard to things inferior to it. The first is nothing but turning to contemplate its Father. The second, likewise, is nothing but knowing itself. The last is turning itself to the production and care of this sensible world, which is produced by it as we said above.

These three operations are understood to proceed from that Mind in such a way that by virtue of that part of it called actuality it turns towards the Father; by virtue of the other, called potentiality, it condescends to the operation of lesser things; by virtue of the two together it fixes its attention on itself. Because of the first two operations it will be called Saturn, because both are contemplative; because of the third, Jupiter. Because this act of producing earthly things is suitable to it because of that nature called potentiality, it is primarily that part of it which is called Jupiter. This is to be observed in what we say in the second book in explaining what the Garden of Jupiter is.

On the same basis, the World-Soul, in so far as it contemplates either itself or things superior to it, can be called Saturn; in so far as it is occupied with the moving and governance of earthly bodies and actions, it is called Jupiter. Because this operation of governing the physical world is especially suited to it, as contemplation is to the Mind, the Mind is called Saturn in an absolute sense and the World-Soul Jupiter, although that Mind, every time it is spoken of as maker of the world, is called Jupiter for the reason given above. This is the true and proper use of these names.

[1]26c.
[2]Fons Vitae IV, 5-6.

Chapter Ten

Of the composition, division, and order of this sensible world, and the reason why it is said to be divided among the three sons of Saturn.

This world, therefore, is produced by that Mind in the image of the intelligible world produced in itself by the first Father, and it is composed, like every animal, of a soul and a body. The body of the world is all that which appears to our eyes, made, as is written in the Timaeus[1], of the four elements: fire, air, water, earth. For a true understanding of this, it is necessary to recall the basic principle we spoke of in the first chapter: that everything has three modes of being, causal, formal, and participated.

The four elements, therefore, must also have these three modes of being. The first, causal being, they have in the heavenly bodies, because the substance of these bodies is not composed of this fire, water, air, and earth which are commonly called the four elements down here under the moon, but they contain them all as every cause contains its effect, by being the virtue in them which is productive of lesser bodies. It is not in any way to be thought that the body of the sky is a substance composed of these elements, as other bodies are on our level, because, besides reasons adduced by others, it would follow, that this part of the world from the moon on down existed before the higher, heavenly part, because the simple elements in themselves are understood to exist first and only later, as a consequence of their coming together, that which is compounded from them.

In the heavens therefore the elements have their causal being, as Plato would have it[2] and not their formal, as Aristotle correctly denies. Of this we shall speak at more length elsewhere. From the moon to the earth they have their formal being, and their third mode of being, the participated, diminished and imperfect, in the subterranean parts. That this is true, that fire, air, and water are found in the bowels of the earth, experience demonstrates, the natural philosophers prove, and the ancient theologians confirm, designating the elements enigmatically by the names of the four infernal rivers, Acheron, Cocytus, Styx, and Phlegethon.

Therefore we can divide the body of the world into three parts, heavenly, earthly, and infernal, using the second two names in the common way also used by the ancients, which is to call this part from the moon down the world proper, because of which John the Evangelist, speaking of the souls which are infused into bodies by God, says "every man who comes into the world"[3], and thus it is used in many other places. Likewise they call the subterranean part Hell, reckoned by many as a place of punishment for noxious souls. From this it can be understood why the realm of Saturn is said by the poets to be divided among his three sons, Jupiter, Neptune, and Pluto. This denotes nothing but the threefold variety of this physical world, both of its body, in the manner said, and also of the World-Soul, according to how we understand these three different parts to be animated by it.

The realm of Saturn is the intelligible world, the archetype of this one, which, while it remains Saturn's -- that is, while it remains in its ideal and intelligible state -- remains one and undivided and consequently more strong and stable. When it came into the hands of his sons, transmuted into physical being, and divided by them into three parts according to the variety of that threefold being, it became weaker and a great deal less powerful than it was at first, degenerating just as any corporeal thing degenerates from the spiritual. They say that the first part, the sky, was Jupiter's, the last and lowest Pluto's, the middle Neptune's. Because this part is the one where generation and corruption chiefly occur, it is symbolized for theologians by water and the sea, which is in continual ebb and flow, so that by Heraclitus this continuous motion of generated and corruptible things is likened to the motion of a swift torrent.[4] For this reason the poets say that the kingdom of the sea is ruled by Neptune, and by Neptune the theologians in their mysteries mean that power, or rather divinity, which presides over generation.

Although it is not necessary for our purpose, still, because it occurs to me as I write, I shall not refrain from expounding the principle of the creation of the world according to Moses as a statement and confirmation of what we have said, that is, that all that part from the moon to the earth is signified by water. Moses says that in the beginning God created heaven and earth and that the earth was empty and void, and darkness was upon the face of the deep, and the spirit of God moved upon the waters, and God said, "Let there be light."⁵ We explain these words in our fashion thus: God first created the heavens and the earth, and the earth was empty and void, without plants, or animals, or other things, because these things are born on the earth only by virtue of the heavenly light and the rays from the superior bodies which descend upon it. Moses adds the reason why the earth was empty and void: the darkness was upon the deep. This was because the heavenly light did not yet descend upon the sphere of the moon, within which the above-mentioned things are generated by its virtue.

We do not have to suppose that there are three different souls which form and rule these three parts of the world, because, the world being one, it should have only one Soul. This, to the extent that it animates and vivifies the subterranean parts of the world, is called Pluto. To the extent that it vivifies the part under the moon it is called Neptune. To the extent that it vivifies the heavens, it is called Jupiter. Therefore Plato says in the <u>Philebus</u> that by Jupiter is understood a ruling soul, that part of the World-Soul which is the chief and rules and dominates the others.⁶ Although by others this division among the three sons of Saturn may have been explained differently, I have chosen to relate only that which is my own opinion and which I consider most true, omitting the explanations adduced by the Greeks, all of which we shall examine elsewhere. For a more perfect knowledge of the things mentioned, the nature of the heavenly bodies and the earthly elements, I wish to mention that according to most of the Platonists the heavenly bodies, like others, are composed of matter and form, although of more perfect matter of a different sort.

[1] 48b, ff.
[2] Idem.
[3] 1:9
[4] Fr. 12
[5] Genesis 1:1-3.
[6] 30c-d.

Chapter Eleven

That the souls of the eight heavenly spheres, together with the World-Soul, are the nine Muses.

Along with the World-Soul the Platonists posit many other rational souls, among which are eight principal ones, the souls of the heavenly spheres, which according to the ancients were no more than eight,[1] the seven planets and the sphere of the fixed stars. These are the nine Muses celebrated by the poets, among whom the first is Calliope, who is the Soul of the world in general, and the other eight are distributed in order, each to her own sphere. Therefore we ought to say that Calliope is the noblest and foremost of all souls and the Soul of the whole world in general.

[1] Medieval thought, as in Dante, added the crystalline sphere, or primum mobile, and the empyrean.

Chapter Twelve

Of the World-Soul in general and of all the other rational souls and of the harmonious adjustment which man has with all the parts of the world

Plato writes in the _Timaeus_ that in the same mixing bowl and of the same elements the fabricator of the world made the World-Soul and all other rational souls[1], among which, as the universal World-Soul is the most perfect, so ours are the last and most imperfect, of whose parts we shall take brief note. Man, like a chain and knot for the world, is placed in the middle of the universe. As every man parrticipates in its extremes, so through his different parts man has communion and harmony with all parts of the world, for which reason he is commonly called a little world, a microcosm.

First in the world we see physical nature, which is of two kinds. One is eternal, the substance of the heavens, the other corruptible, as are the elements and everything composed of them, like stars, metals, and such things. Then there are the plants; third, the dumb animals; fourth, the rational animals; fifth, the Angelic Mind, above which is God, fountain and source of all created being. Likewise, as we shall prove in our debate, there are, according to the opinion of Aristotle and Plato, two bodies in man: one eternal, called by the Platonists the heavenly vehicle, which is immediately vivified by the rational soul, the other corruptible, which we see with our bodily eyes, composed of the four elements. In it there is the vegetative soul, through which this corruptible body is fed, nourished, and grows, and that eternal one lives an everlasting life. Thirdly there is the sensitive and motive part, in which man resembles the irrational animals.[2] Fourthly, there is the rational part, which is peculiar to man and to rational animals and by the Latin Peripatetics is believed to be the last and most noble part of our souls, although there is nonetheless above it the intellectual and angelic part, in which man is like the angels, even though in the sensitive part he is like the animals.

The pinnacle of this intellectual part the
Platonists call the unity of the soul, and they hold
it to be that through which man is immediately united
with God and, as it were, linked to Him, as in the
vegetative part he is linked to the plants.   As to
which of these parts of the soul are immortal and
which mortal, there is disagreement among the
Platonists.   Proclus and Porphyry will have it that
only the rational part is immortal and all the others
are corruptible.   Xenocrates and Speusippus make the
sensitive part immortal also.   Numenius[3] and
Plotinus, adding even the vegetative part, conclude
every soul to be immortal.

[1]41d.
[2]It is hard to see why Pico says "thirdly", as
he seems to be talking about the three Aristotelian
levels of soul, which I have supplied in the
preceding sentence.   If the parts referred to are
bodily parts, the next sentence does not seem to fit.
Stanley's translation takes the vegetative soul as
second to the corruptible body in this sequence.
[3]2nd century Greek Syrian Platonist, forerunner
of Plotinus.

Chapter Thirteen, and Last of the First Book

Of the Ideas and their threefold being.

The Ideas celebrated by the Platonists are both the most useful and the most difficult of all the topics discussed by the philosophers, and in our debate and in our commentary on Plato's Symposium we shall treat precisely of these, on which depends the way in which the Angels, our souls, and the heavenly souls possess knowledge.

The Greek Platonists treat of all these matters briefly and obscurely, so that perhaps our words will not be useless to students of Platonism. For our own purposes, however, noting certain compendious statements of theirs, we shall make an end to our first book, introducing the treatise on love which follows. We shall have to remember the first principle which we proposed in the first chapter, that everything has a threefold mode of being, causal, formal, and participated. There must therefore be a similar being of the Ideas, which will have causal being in God, formal in the Angelic Mind, and participated in the Rational Soul. In God, according to the Platonists, Ideas do not exist, but He is the cause and beginning of all Ideas, which He produces first in the Angelic Mind, as is also clearly found in the Chaldean Oracles[1]. By that Angelic Mind in turn, the Rational Soul is made a participant in them.

On that account, when our soul turns to its intellectual and angelic part, it is illuminated by it, participating in the true Forms of things, which, just as in the intellect they are called Ideas, so, when they are in the soul, are called not Ideas but concepts. In this respect the souls of corruptible bodies like ours and some demons' are, according to the Platonists, different from the heavenly souls because the heavenly ones do not, in the administration of their bodies, separate themselves from their intellectual parts but, always conversant and united with them, perform both functions, contemplation and the governance of the body.

28

Therefore the Platonists say that bodies rise to
them, not that they descend into bodies. Other
souls, assigned to the care of short-lived and
earthly bodies, are deprived of intellectual
contemplation and seek knowledge of things through
their senses, to which they are completely
predisposed and therefore always full of many errors
and false opinions. From this prison and
wretchedness we shall see below that love is a very
potent means of escape, which through the beauty of
physical and sensible things arouses in the soul a
memory of its intellectual part and is the occasion
for returning to it from earthly life, truly a dream
of a shadow, as Pindar writes[2], bringing that soul to
eternal life, where purged, as it were, by the fire
of love, as we shall show in the following work, it
is most happily transmuted into angelic form.

[1]Prophetic writings in Aramaic, mistakenly
thought in the Middle Ages to be the language of
ancient Chaldea or Babylonia. Possibly in the books
of Ezra and Daniel, or in Aramaic paraphrases of
other Hebrew prophets. For the oracular reputation
of the Chaldeans or Babylonians in ancient times, cf.
Horace, Odes, I, xi.
[2]Pyth. 8, 136.

HERE FOLLOWS THE SECOND BOOK
OF THE MOST ILLUSTRIOUS LORD COUNT
GIOVANNI PICO DELLA MIRANDOLA
ON THE ABOVE POEM.

Chapter One

That every time that the name of the thing meant is ambiguous, that which is signified by such a name ought first to be explained.

Plato says in many places, and Aristotle after him, and also every other school of philosophers, that in treating of any subject one should first state what the name of the thing under discussion signifies. To carry out this aim, they demand that every time the name is equivocal, meaning various and different things, we ought to distinguish these meanings and say for which one we intend primarily to use it. Not doing this may make every discussion confused, disorderly, and vain, and from nowhere else came the errors of Sophists, whom Plato reproaches in so many of his dialogues, than from not following this rule of distinguishing equivocal and ambiguous terms. Eudemus[1] holds Plato to have been the first inventor of this rule. On this account, whoever without logic, in which the above method is learned, has put or, indeed, puts his hands to philosophical matters, especially Platonic ones, is bound to fill both himself and whoever listens to his words with infinite errors and the greatest confusion. Since this word love, as we shall see in the following chapter, is commonly used to signify various things, it is necessary before we speak of love, to say what is here intended by this word, excluding everything else which it could mean.

[1]Probably Aristotle's pupil Eudemus of Rhodes.

Chapter Two

Of this word "love" and its different meanings.

Just as the cognitive powers of the soul revolve around the true and the false, so do the appetitive powers around the good and the bad. The cognitive power gives its assent to what it judges to be true and dissents from what it judges to be false. By philosophers such assent is called affirmation, and such dissent negation. Likewise the power of the soul which desires inclines towards what presents itself to it with the appearance of good, and withdraws and flees from what has the appearance of evil. That inclination is called love, that flight and withdrawal, hate.

This is the broadest and most general meaning of the word <u>love</u> which can be given, and under this fall many kinds, which differ among themselves according to the diversity of the goods towards which our desire is inclined. If this love is for wealth, for example, and especially if it is inordinate, it is called avarice; if for honor, ambition. Likewise, if it is for the gods or maybe a parent, it would be called piety; if for someone equal, it would be called friendship.

Excluding these and all the other meanings, we are concerned only with the desire to possess what either is or seems to us beautiful. So love is defined by Plato in the <u>Symposium</u>: desire of the beautiful.[1] As saying "the poet" is understood among the Greeks to refer to Homer, and among us to Virgil, from their excellence above all other poets, so saying "love" in an absolute sense is understood to refer to love of beauty, certainly to what excels and surpasses every desire for any other created thing. The same is seen in the Latin language, in which, although it is properly said that someone loves God, someone his brother, and someone money, nevertheless, when saying simply that someone loves, it is understood that he is ensnared by the love of somebody's beauty, which is popularly called "being in love." And since among all desires and loves this love of beauty is the most ardent, Plato says in the <u>Phaedrus</u> that it is called love a <u>romis</u>[2], which in Greek means what <u>strength</u> and <u>vehemence</u> do in the

32

vulgar tongue. For this reason every time we wish to signify that some other love or desire is vehement we distinguish it by some phrase, as such a one is said to be in love with letters, such a one with arms, etc.

Therefore both Plato in the Symposium[3] and the Phaedrus[4] and our Poet in the present poem speak of the love in which whoever is caught in it is popularly said to be, the love which is nothing but the desire to enjoy and possess the beauty of another person. From this it is concluded that both the love with which God loves His creatures, and that other which is properly called friendship, and many other similar ones are different from this love of which we speak, or even repugnant to it, as in stating the nature of love below we shall clearly show.

It is enough for now to say that since God has no desire for anything outside Himself, being most perfect in everything and lacking nothing, this love of which we speak, the desire to possess the beauty of another, could not be more alien to Him. That love with which He loves His creatures arises from a precisely opposite cause. In the former he who loves needs the beloved thing and receives from it, the beloved, his own completion. In the latter, divine love, the beloved needs the lover, and he who loves gives rather than receives.

Likewise, that love which is called friendship has properties opposite to our love. In friendship reciprocity is always necessary, as Plato says in many places, that is, that each friend love the other in the same way and for the same reason as he is loved by him. And thus conversely, as Plato also says in many places, this is not necessary in our love, because he who loves need not be beautiful and consequently need not be capable of moving the friend to a reciprocal desire for his own beauty.

You can therefore consider, reader, how many
errors our Marsilio committed in his first commentary
under this head alone, perverting what Plato says of
love, although in addition, in every part of his
treatise, he has made mistakes on every subject, as I
believe will be clearly shown in due course.

[1] 201a.
[2] 238c.
[3] 201a.
[4] 238c.

Chapter Three

The love of which we are speaking, therefore,
can be defined as Plato defines it, as the desire for
beauty. <u>Desire</u> is used here to refer to the generic
and common nature which love shares with all other
desires, just as man, in so far as he is an animal,
is like all the wild beasts. Then <u>for beauty</u> is
added to specify the particular kind of love and to
distinguish it from other desires, as man is
distinguished from other animals by being rational
and mortal. Therefore if we understand perfectly the
parts of this definition we shall perfectly
understand love.

Beginning with the first part, I say that desire
is nothing but the inclination and impulse of him who
desires towards that which either is or seems to him
to be advantageous to him. Such a thing is called
good. Therefore the object of desire is the good,
either real or apparent. As there are different
kinds of good, so there arise different kinds of
desire, as for our purpose love, which is a kind of
desire, is for that kind of good which is called the
beautiful. From this we conclude that the beautiful
is distinct from the good as a species is from its
genus and not as an extrinsic thing is from an
intrinsic one, as Marsilio says.

Chapter Four

What natural desire is.

Desire can at the first division be divided into two kinds, natural desire and desire based on knowledge. For a full comprehension of natural desire, it is to be understood that, the object of desire being the good, and every creature having some perfection proper to it for participation in the divine goodness, from which what proceeded was, as Moses writes[1], very good, each creature must have a definite end in which it finds that degree of happiness of which it is capable and towards which it naturally tends, just as everything heavy tends towards the center.

This tendency, in creatures which do not have knowledge, is called natural desire, a great testimony to the divine providence by which creatures such as these are directed towards their ends as an archer's arrow is towards the target, which is not known by the arrow but is known by him who with the eye of wisest foresight shoots it towards that target. With this desire God is desired by all creatures, because, since every particular good is a vestige and instance of the first good, which is God Himself, in every good which is desired He is the first desideratum.

The good of stones and plants is nothing but what they are capable of sharing of the divine goodness, and just as a nature is capable of participating more or less, so it is ordained to a more or to a less noble end. On this account the end of all creatures is the same, to enjoy God in the way possible to them and to taste as much as they can of the sweetness of His excellence. According to their power of achieving it, however, their ends are more or less diversified. From this you will understand how God is that good, of which Aristotle speaks in the beginning of his Ethics[2], which all things desire, and you will know from what is said there both how they desire it, although not knowing it, and how they do not desire anything impossible to them. How far from the truth is the opinion of those who

have otherwise interpreted Aristotle here, we shall
show elsewhere with the clearest reasons.   Turning
towards God with this natural desire, every creature
praises and adores Him, as the Hebrew prophets sing[3]
and as if beseeching Him all address and offer
themselves to Him, as the great Platonist Theodore[4]
writes.

[1] Genesis 1:25.
[2] I, 1, 1094a.
[3] Cf. Psalms 145:10.
[4] Probably Theodore Gaza, a 15th century
Byzantine scholar active in Italy, though he seems to
have been more an Aristotelian than a Platonist.

Chapter Five

Of desire in general and how, in itself, it is
always directed towards the good.

The other kind of desire does not exist except
for things known by the one who desires.   It is
established by nature that to every cognitive faculty
there should be joined an appetitive one which loves
and embraces what the cognitive judges to be good and
hates and rejects what it judges to be evil.   This
appetitive faculty, so far as it is determined by its
own nature, is always directed towards the good, and
there was never anyone who wished to be miserable.
Because the cognitive faculty is often mistaken in
its judgment, however, and judges that to be good
which is really evil, it happens that sometimes the
appetitive faculty, which in itself is blind and
unknowing, does desire evil.   On the one hand it can
be said that it does so voluntarily, because no one
can do violence to it, but on the other hand it can
be said that it does not do so voluntarily, because
it does so only when deceived by the judgment of its
partner and by itself would never desire evil.   Plato
understands this in the Timaeus when he says that no
one sins voluntarily.[1]

[1] 86d.

36

Chapter Six

That to know things is one way of possessing them.

There follows a property common to every faculty of desire, and this is that whoever desires always in part possesses the thing desired and in part not, and if he were completely deprived of its possession he would never desire it. This can be verified in two ways. The first is that, as was said in the last chapter, the thing is not desired unless it is known, and it is said subtly by the philosophers that to know things is one way of possessing them, from which follows that popular saying of Aristotle that our souls are all things because they know all things[1], and in Asaph, the Hebrew poet, God says "All things are mine because I know them all"[2], although just as there is a great difference between His knowledge and ours, so likewise is there one in the mode of possession.

The other way is that between him who desires and the thing desired there is always a correspondence and likeness. Everything rejoices at, and preserves itself by, what is most suitable to it by natural affinity; by what is dissimilar and contrary to it, it is saddened and corrupted. Therefore love does not occur between unlikes, and the repugnance of two opposed natures is nothing other than a natural hatred, as hatred is nothing other than repugnance based on knowledge. From this it clearly follows that it is necessary that the nature of the desired object be somehow found in the one who desires, because otherwise there would be no likeness between them, and that it be found there imperfectly, because it would be vain to seek for what is fully possessed.

[1] De Anima, III, 3, 427a.
[2] Cf. Psalms 50:10-11.

Chapter Seven

That to different cognitive natures are annexed different appetitive natures.

As desire in general follows knowledge, so to different types of knowledge are annexed different types of desire, and this is enough for now. If knowledge operates on three levels, sense, reason, and intellect, on these there follow likewise three grades of desire, which could be called appetite, choice, and will. Appetite follows on sense, choice on reason, will on intellect. Appetite exists in brute beasts, choice in men and in every other nature which is found between us and the angels, and just as sense knows nothing but corporeal and sensible things, so appetite desires nothing but corporeal and sensible goods, and as the angelic intellect is intent only on the contemplation of spiritual concepts and has no inclination towards material things except in so far as, already released and set free from matter, they become immaterial and spiritual, so its will feeds itself on incorporeal and spiritual goods. The rational nature, placed between these two as a mean between extremes, now leaning towards one side, sense, now rising towards the other, intellect, can by its choice follow a desire for either.

From all these things it can be concluded that every time that the thing desired is a corporeal and sensible thing the desire for it must be either an appetite following on sensation or a choice of reason inclined towards sensation. Every time that the thing desired is incorporeal and non-sensible the desire must be either an intellectual and angelic will or a rational choice raised and elevated to the sublimity of intellect. Love, therefore, having been seen to be a desire, and what desire is having been stated, in order to know what kind of desire love may be, whether sensitive, rational, or intellectual, which is as much as to say whether bestial, human, or angelic, it is necessary to see what beauty is, which is the object of such a desire. This known, we shall have an absolute knowledge of the definition of love, and consequently of love itself.

Chapter Eight

Of beauty in general.

The word beauty can be taken in a broad and general sense, and it can be taken this way every time that two or more different things come together in the composition of a third which arises from their proper mixture and just proportion. The elegance that results from this proportioned mingling is called beauty. Since every created thing is composite and may be composed in as correct a ratio and proportion as is possible to a thing of that nature, every created thing can, in this way, be called beautiful, this beauty being nothing but that proper proportioning which is the reason why these natures, although varied and different, still combine and join together to compose a single whole. For this reason nothing simple can be beautiful. From this it follows that there is no beauty in God, because beauty involves the imperfection of being somehow composite. This is not at all suitable for the First Cause, in which for this reason the Platonists do not place the Ideas, since there is in Him no variety whether real or imaginary, but a supreme and inestimable simplicity, as was said in the first book.

Below Him begins beauty, because contrariety begins, without which there can be no created things, but there would be only God. This contrariety and discord of diverse natures is not enough to constitute a creature unless through proper proportion the contrariety becomes unified and the discord concordant, which can be assigned as a true definition of beauty, that it is nothing other than a friendly enmity and a concordant discord. Heraclitus therefore called war and strife the father and progenitor of all things[1], and in Homer whoever speaks ill of strife is said to have blasphemed against nature.

Empedocles spoke more perfectly, however, taking discord not by itself but along with harmony as the beginning of things[2], meaning by discord the variety of the natures of which they are composed, and by harmony their union. He therefore said that only in God is there no discord, because in Him there is no union of diverse natures but rather a simple unity without any composition. Because in the constitution of creatures it is necessary that unity overcome contrariety, or otherwise the thing will dissolve because its components will separate from each other, it is said by the poets that Venus loves Mars, because the beauty that is called Venus, as we shall see below, does not exist without that contrariety, and they say that Venus tames and softens Mars because that just proportion restricts and smooths over the conflict and hatred which exist between contrary natures.

Likewise, according to the ancient astrologers, whose opinion follows that of Plato and Aristotle and even Moses, according to what Abenaza the Spaniard[3] writes, Venus was placed in the middle of the sky near Mars in order that she might tame his violence, which by its nature is destructive and corrupting, just as Jupiter tames the malice of Saturn. If Mars were always subject to Venus, the contrariety of the component parts to their just proportion, nothing would ever break down.

[1] Fr. 44.
[2] Fr. 17.
[3] Probably Abenezra of Toledo, 1093-1167, Jewish grammarian and commentator on the Pentateuch.

Chapter Nine

Of beauty strictly taken.

This is the broad and general meaning of beauty, in which this word implies harmony, wherefore God is said to have composed the whole world with musical and harmonic proportions.[1] Just as harmony can be taken generally for the proper proportioning of every compound thing, however, yet strictly signifies only the tempering of many voices coming together in one melody, so too, although beauty can be attributed to everything properly composed, nevertheless its proper application is to visible things only, just as that of harmony is to audible things. This beauty is that for which the desire is called love.

Therefore beauty is born from a single cognitive power, namely sight, and so it was always celebrated by Musaeus[2] and Propertius and by all the Greek and Latin poets in general. Plotinus is influenced by this to believe that the name Eros, which in Greek means love, is derived from the term orasis, which means vision.

But, someone will say, if beauty lies only in the things which are perceived by sight, how can it be attributed to the Ideas, which are by their nature wholly invisible? In the statement of this doubt, on which the foundation of this subject rests, it is to be noted that there are two kinds of sight, the one corporeal and the other incorporeal. The first is that which is commonly called sight, which Aristotle says is loved by us above all the other senses. The other is that power of the soul in which, in the next to last chapter of the first book, it was said that we are like the angels. This power is called sight by all the Platonists, and corporeal vision is nothing but a copy of it. Aristotle, in his Ethics and many other places, says that the intellect has the same relation to the soul as sight to the body. Therefore, in Homer, Pallas, who represents intellectual wisdom, boasts above all of the beauty of her eyes. With this sight Moses, Paul, and many of the other elect saw the face of God. This is what

41

our theologians call intellectual cognition,
intuitive cognition. With this sight John the
Evangelist says that the just will see God Almighty[3],
and that this will be our whole reward.

[1]An echo of Pythagoras.
[2]Cf. Hero and Leander, 11. 92-95.
[3]Cf. I John 1:9.

Chapter Ten

That strictly taken there are two beauties,
physical beauty and intellectual beauty.

Beauty being therefore in visible things and
there being two forms of vision, the one corporeal
and the other incorporeal, there will also be two
kinds of visible objects and consequently two kinds
of beauty. These are the two Venuses celebrated by
Plato[1] and by our Poet, namely the corporeal and
sensible beauty, called the vulgar Venus, and the
intelligible beauty which is in the Ideas, which, as
we showed above, is an object of the intellect, as
colors are of sight, and which is called the heavenly
Venus. Love being the appetite for beauty, it
follows from this that just as there are two beauties
there necessarily have to be two loves, vulgar and
heavenly, such that the former desires the vulgar and
sensible beauty, the latter the heavenly and
intelligible. Therefore Plato said in the Symposium
that there are necessarily as many loves as there are
Venuses.

[1]Symposium 140d.

Chapter Eleven

Why Venus, or beauty, is said to be the mother of Love.

It is not, therefore, by any power of the soul
or mind but beauty that Love is generated, and Venus
is deservedly said to be his mother. Because beauty
is the cause of love, not as the productive principle
of the act but as its object, and according to the
Platonists the soul is the efficient cause of its
activities, and their objectives are like the matter
from which the soul produces that actuality, beauty
thus coming to be the material cause of Love, Venus
is said to be his mother, because by the philosophers
the material cause is likened to the mother, as the
efficient to the father, referring to whom by Vulcan,
the blacksmith and arteficer of the physical world,
the theologians say that Venus was married to him
because of the great beauty which appears in the
workmanship of this world. All presuppose this as a
known thing, on which Marsilio had to take pains not
to err, because on this depends almost the whole
subject, and whoever is mistaken on this must be not
a little distant from the truth in all its other
aspects.

Chapter Twelve

Brief epilogue on Venus, Love, and the Ideas.

Venus will therefore be that beauty which
engenders love. The heavenly and ideal beauty
engenders the heavenly love, which will be defined
thus: heavenly love is the intellectual desire for
ideal beauty. It was stated above what appetite is
and what intellectual appetite is. In the sixth
chapter of the first book we spoke of the Ideas,
which, to put it briefly, are nothing but the
exemplary Forms of the natures of things, and every
intellect is full of them, and it understands by
means of those of which it is written in the Book of
Causes[1] that every intelligence is full of Forms.

43

In the last chapter of the first book it was said that in God, as in their fountain and source, these Forms are called Ideas. In their essence they are in the Angelic Mind, in which they were first produced by God. Finally, by participation, they are in the Rational Soul. Just as it participates in the substance of the Intellect, so it participates in those Ideas and consequently in their beauty. From this we can conclude the love of the beauty of the soul to be, not yet perfect heavenly love, but its near and perfect image, which first is found in the appetite for ideal beauty, which necessarily resides in the first Mind, which without intermediary God clothes and adorns with the beauty of the Ideas.

[1]Neo-Platonic treatise drawn largely from Proclus' Elements of Theology, translated into Latin via Arabic, and long attributed to Aristotle, though probably not by Pico's time.

Chapter Thirteen

Of the birth of Love and what is meant by the Garden of Jupiter, by Porus, and by Penia, and by the birthday of Venus.

Plato says that Love was born in the Garden of Jupiter, on the birthday of Venus, Porus having married Penia, with all the gods present at the wedding feast, and Porus, the son of Prudence, being drunk with nectar.[1] Love was previously supposed to be the uncreated god and creator of everything else.[2] In this fashion we must understand that formless nature which, shaped by God, makes up the Angelic Mind, as was said in the ninth chapter of the first book. The Form which God gives to the Angelic Mind is nothing but the Ideas, which, as we said, are the first beauty. Therefore the Ideas descend into the Angelic Mind from God, and because everything which moves away from its source and beginning and mixes with a contrary nature becomes less perfect, the Ideas, distancing themselves from God, their fount and beginning, and joining themselves to that formless nature, wholly unlike their own shapeliness, necessarily become imperfect. Therefore the Angelic

Mind has in itself the beauty of the Ideas, but imperfectly, because of the opacity of its own shadowy substance. From this there necessarily follows in it the desire to attain their perfection. This desire, being the desire for beauty, is the one which by us is called love, which would not arise if the Ideas either were not in the Angelic Mind at all or were there in their perfection. As we said in the fourth chapter of this book, the thing desired is partly possessed and partly not, and if the lover were completely different from the thing loved there would not be any of that likeness between them which is the cause of love.

Love, then, is born when Porus, which means plenty, the confluence of the Ideas, is mixed with that formless nature called Penia because it is poor and beggarly, being deprived of all being and actuality. Properly speaking, Penia is not the essence of that formless nature, but only its imperfection and indigence. The formless nature, we said in the eighth chapter of the first book, was called Jupiter, and we explained why. Here it is called the Garden of Jupiter, because the Ideas are planted in it like trees in a garden. From this it comes about that the Angelic Mind, already adorned with those Ideas, was then called "paradise" by the ancients, which is a Greek word and means what garden does to us. All those who were living the intellectual life and, raised above human nature like the angels, nourished themselves on contemplation, were said to be in paradise. Exhorting us to this contemplative life and eternal happiness, Zoroaster exclaims, "Seek out, seek out Paradise!"

This term has later been used by our own theologians to mean also a physical place, the highest heaven, which is the abode and habitation of the souls of the blessed, whose blessedness consists in contemplation and in the perfection of the intellect, as Plato in both the Philebus and the Epinomis says as openly as this opinion is held and defended by many of our own theologians, like Scotus, Egidius[3], and many others.

The Garden of Jupiter is therefore that formless
essence, and in it, from the perfection of the Ideas
which is Porus, joined to its own imperfection and
perfect lack of being, which arise from the imperfect
nature of that essence, was born Love, the desire for
their perfection. Love was not born until the
birthday of Venus, not until ideal beauty, though
imperfect, was born in the Angelic Mind. To speak of
the birth of Venus is as much as if Venus were said
to be imperfect, as it were, and different from
perfect beauty, as a child in swaddling clothes is
from an adult in her prime.

On the birthday of Venus all the gods were
seated at the banquet; here is to be remembered what
was said in the sixth chapter of the first book, that
besides its own natural being everything has another
mode of being called ideal, in accordance with what
was produced by God in the first Mind. Thus by
"Saturn" can be understood both the planet Saturn and
the Idea of Saturn, and so of all the rest. Here by
the gods we must understand, as will be more clear in
Chapter XXIII of this book, the Ideas of all the
gods, and in this Plato follows the mode of speech of
Parmenides the Pythagorean, who always calls the
Ideas gods. The gods are therefore the Ideas, which
preceded Venus, because she is that elegance and
grace which result from the variety of these Ideas,
and it is said that they were at the banquet because
their father was then feasting them on nectar and
ambrosia.

By this one must understand that the ancient
theologians, as Hesiod writes and Aristotle confirms,
are saying that all those things which God fed with
nectar and ambrosia at His table are eternal. Other
things, which are not eternal, were not present at
that banquet. Therefore, the Ideas of the Angelic
Mind being both first and truly eternal, Plato writes
that they were present at the heavenly banquet where
they were fed with nectar and ambrosia, saying still
more expressly that Porus, the universal confluence
of the Ideas, had gotten drunk on nectar. Therefore,
however many Ideas of other things there may be, he
nevertheless does not say that they were admitted to
the banquet, because they were not granted the gift
of immortality.

I believe I have now adequately told how Love
was born in the Garden of Jupiter from the meeting of
Porus and Penia, at the banquet on the birthday of
Venus, with the gods sitting at the table and
feasting.

[1] Symposium 203b-c.
[2] Symposium 178a.
[3] Commentator on Aristotle's logical works, d.
1316.

Chapter Fourteen

Why Love is placed by Orpheus in the womb of Chaos

From the things said above, it is clear why Love
is placed by Orpheus in the womb of Chaos rather than
in that of any god, since chaos means nothing but
matter filled with all the Forms, but confusedly and
imperfectly. Therefore when the Angelic Mind was
already full of all the Ideas, but they were still
imperfect and rather indistinct and confused, that
Mind in which Love, the desire for their perfection,
was born could be called Chaos.

Chapter Fifteen

For what sort of thing the word "circle" is appropriate and why.

The Angelic Mind therefore wishes to make those
Ideas perfect, and it is reasonable that their
perfection should arise from a cause opposite to that
of their imperfection. Their imperfection comes from
two causes. One is their separation from their fount
and source; the other is their union with a different
and contrary nature. Therefore their perfection will
come both from removing and separating themselves
from that dissimilar nature and from returning whence
they first proceeded, reuniting themselves as closely
as they can with their source.

On this account love, the desire to acquire this beauty, stirs and stimulates the Angelic Mind to turn towards God and to join itself to Him as closely as it can, because each thing achieves perfection to the extent that it rejoins its source. This is the first circle, the Angelic Mind, which, proceeding from the indivisible unity of God, completely returns there by a circular motion of intrinsic intelligence. Every nature which is able to do this is called a circle, because the circular figure returns to the same point from which it started.

This property is found in only two natures, the angelic and the rational. For this same reason only these two natures are capable of felicity, because felicity is nothing but coming to one's highest good and ultimate end, and the ultimate end of everything is the same as its first beginning. Therefore those natures which can return to their first principle again can achieve felicity, and such alone are the immortal substances, because corporeal and material natures do not possess, as all the Peripatetic and Platonic philosophers agree, this power which they call reflexive, by means of which they can return either into themselves or to their source. Only from their cause, therefore, do they proceed and participate in that good which from their cause is communicated to them. Not being able to reunite this good with its source, they cannot achieve absolute perfection, but their good always remains imperfect. On this account they lack felicity, or possess it so imperfectly that it cannot properly be called felicity. There being therefore only two natures, the angelic and the rational, which can return to their source, only these two can be called circles, and they ought to be called intelligible circles because they are not material.

Likewise among bodies, according to our own theologians, there are two circles, copies and images of these. One is the tenth heaven, which is a corporeal and motionless circle[1], an image of the intelligible circle which is the Angelic Mind. The other circle is the body of the heavens, the moving image of that circle which is the Rational Soul. Of the first the Platonists make no mention, and would perhaps say that the angelic nature, being wholly separate and different from corporeal nature and not having any abode in it, cannot be represented by any

48

corporeal thing. Of the second Plato makes express
mention in the Timaeus, showing how all the circles
of the moving heavenly bodies, which are divided by
him into the sphere of the fixed stars and the seven
planets, are images of just as many immaterial
circles in the rational soul.[2]

Some apply the word circle to God, and this
seems the opinion of the ancient theologians who call
Him heaven, as if He were a sphere comprehending all
things in itself, as the outermost heaven comprehends
all corporeal things in itself. It is not unfitting
for the term circle, according to one argument, to be
applied to Him nor, according to another, for it to
be repugnant to Him. Understanding by a circle, as
we have explained above, a nature which, starting
from an indivisible point, returns to the same one,
the term is utterly inapplicable to God, who in this
sense is not a circle, because He does not have His
beginning from elsewhere but is Himself the
indivisible point from which all circles begin and to
which they all return, so that, as regards this
property, the term circle is repugnant to God,
because He has neither beginning nor end. It is
repugnant also to material things because, although
they begin with one source, they cannot return to it.
It remains that it be proper to the mind and the
soul.

According to many others however, this term is
suitable to God, first because it is the most perfect
figure of all, as God is the most perfect of all
things, and only to this figure can no addition be
made, which shows it to be absolutely perfect.
Another reason comes in, which I believe to be the
most important: that the final sphere is the location
of everything which is located. The Platonists
subtly prove this of God by declaring, as Porphyry
does among others, that the soul is not in the body,
as it seems to the vulgar, which Plato also notes in
the Timaeus[3], but on the contrary it is the body
which is in the soul, and for the same reason the
Soul is in the Angelic Mind and the Angelic Mind in
God, the outermost place of all places, which can be
understood from the mysteries of the Hebrews, who
among the most holy names of God include this one,
Place, and so He is often called by them in the holy
scriptures. Therefore for this reason, to state
which sufficiently would require more words but would

be beyond our purpose, and for those reasons given
above, God will be called a circle, which is
especially to be observed in the theology of the
Ishmaelites[4], not that of Parmenides[5], though many
think so. We shall prove elsewhere that what he
calls the intelligible sphere is not God but the
intelligible world immediately produced by God.

[1]It is worth noting here the contrast with
Dante, for whom the tenth heaven, though motionless,
is the intelligible empyrean, not a material body.
[2]34b.
[3]34c
[4]Arabs
[5]Frs. 8, 42.

Chapter Sixteen

Brief epilogue on the birth of Love.

    As an epilogue, therefore, I shall say briefly
that on the day when Venus was born, that is, when
the beauty of the Ideas first descended into the
Angelic Mind, Venus being newly born and not yet
adult, that is, that beauty being still imperfect,
Love was also born, that is, there arose in the
Angelic Mind the desire to possess completely that
beauty which in some sense it already had, and
stimulated by this love it turned to God and from Him
received the perfection of that ideal beauty. Since
He had this completely in Himself, Venus in Him was
already full-grown and come to her perfection.

Chapter Seventeen

Of the three Graces attending Venus, and their names.

The poets say that this Venus has for her attendants and handmaidens the three Graces, and their names in the vulgar tongue are Freshness, Joy, and Brilliance. These three Graces are nothing but three properties resulting from that ideal beauty. First, for a thing to be fresh is nothing but for it to last and remain unimpaired in its being without any corruption. Youth is called fresh because man then has perfect and unimpaired the being which, losing ever more and more of its vigor and soundness with the years, comes to be wholly annihilated, although the being of every composite thing lasts as long as the proper proportions which unite its parts in union with it.

Since Venus is nothing but this proportion, this freshness is surely nothing but a property resulting from Venus. On that account, where the true Venus first has her being, in the ideal world, is found the true freshness of every intelligible nature's being, immutable in its integrity and utterly ageless. This property extends to sensible things so far as they can participate in Venus, because that proportion lasts in them as long as they last and the other two properties of ideal beauty are kept fresh, both the brilliance of the intellect and the motion of the will to desire it, filling that will, once that beauty has been possessed, with unspeakable joy. And because this being, durability, and permanence are not reflexive acts, one of the Graces is depicted with her face towards us as though approaching, not going away; the other two, because they pertain to the intellect and the will, whose operation is reflexive, are depicted looking over their shoulders as though turning around, because these things are said to come to us from the gods and to go back to the gods from us.[1]

[1] I have not been able to find any depiction of the Graces answering to Pico's description. A painting from Stabiae in the National Archeological Museum at Naples carries out the two-to-one contrast, but here the central figure looks over her shoulder while the two flanking ones look to their respective sides.

Chapter Eighteen

Of the birth of Venus, described by the Poets under a veil of fable.

Since Plato says that Love was born on the birthday of Venus, it is necessary now to understand how Venus was born. In the Symposium Plato does not say anything except that she is the daughter of Uranus.[1] Under a veil of fable the ancient theologians of the gentiles tell how she was born of him, saying that Saturn cut off the testicles of his father Uranus and threw them into the sea and that Venus was born from their seed.

For the explanation of this mystery, it is first to be supposed that matter, that formless nature of which we have said every creature is composed, is often represented for the theologians by water, since water is in continuous flux and easily receptive to every form. It would take too long if I tried to bring in all the places, both in the holy Mosaic scriptures and the gospels and in the sacred writings of the gentiles, where this nature is represented by them as water.

[1] 180d

I wish to add only this for comparison, that this formless nature is first found in the Angelic Mind, as in that which is the first creature. On this account the angels are signified by the term "waters", and nothing other than the Angelic Mind is to be understood by the waters that are above the heavens, which David says are continually praising God.[1] Origen Adimantius[2] agrees, and there are some of the Platonists who do not want that Ocean which Homer calls the father of gods and men to be anything but that Angelic Mind, which we said above is the source and fount of every other creature which comes after it. For this reason this first Mind is called Neptune by Georgius Gemistus[3], a highly regarded Platonist, as that which is lord of all the waters, of all the other minds, angelic and human. These are those waters, this that living fountain, from which whoever drinks, never more has thirst. These are the waters and seas upon which, as David says, God has established the world.[4]

[1] Psalms 148:4.
[2] Probably a certain Adimantius, some of whose works were mistakenly attributed to the theologian Origen as early as the 4th century.
[3] Or Gemistus Pletho, c. 1355-1452, Byzantine scholar influential in the development of Platonism among Florentine humanists.
[4] Psalms 136:6.

Chapter Twenty

Explanation of the myth of Saturn.

Secondly we must know why the poets say that Saturn castrated Uranus. In the first part of this work we told how God, who is called Uranus by the Platonists, produced the first angel, which they call the Divine Mind and which the poets call Saturn, and it was said that God Himself did not produce any creature but this, by which the rest of the world was then produced. If, therefore, one who is left sterile and can no longer breed can properly be said to be castrated, then, since the first Angelic Mind is a created thing, if whatever can be communicated by the first God is fully communicated to it in such a way that He no longer remains productive of anything, Saturn is not without good reason said by the poets to castrate his father Uranus.

Saturn therefore castrates Uranus, but Jupiter does not castrate Saturn but rather deprives him of his kingdom, because when the Angelic Mind has produced the World Soul, which is Jupiter, it does not remain barren, as Uranus did after producing Saturn, but produces after it all the heavens and elements and all the other rational souls. Because the administration of these earthly things is carried on through the motion of the heavens and of the Rational Soul, which together move the lesser beings, the World Soul being the beginning of every motion, as we said above, and that Mind being utterly motionless, Saturn is said by the poets to be bound, like one who does not move, and the administration and rule of the world are said to rest with Jupiter, who would therefore not govern the world well if he were not aided by the advice of his aged father. That is, the Soul would not move the heavens in an orderly fashion nor correctly arrange other things if it did not participate in the Father's intellectual wisdom, as is broadly said by Plato[1] in the _Laws_ to whoever reads it with a sound mind. Because his words there were poorly understood both by some Platonists and by all the Manicheans, they have been a source of great error. Thus it should now be

54

clear, however, why Saturn castrated Uranus and Jupiter bound Saturn and took his kingdom from him.

Following this explanation we have adduced, we can say that all those things which Uranus communicated to Saturn, that host of Ideas which descended from God into the Angelic Mind, are the testicles of Uranus, because separated from them he remains barren and no longer productive. These testicles fell into the sea, into the formless angelic nature, and as soon as they were joined with it, Venus was born, who is, as we have said, the beauty resulting from the variety of those Ideas. Because those Ideas would not in themselves have that variety and distinction if they were not mixed with that formless nature, and because without that variety there could be no beauty, it properly follows that Venus could not have been born if the testicles of Uranus has not fallen into the waters of the sea.

[1]896e.

Chapter Twenty-one

<u>Of Porus, and why he is called the son of</u>
<u>Prudence</u>

It remains to say why Porus is called the son of Prudence. Porus being the concourse of Ideas coming from the true God, he is called the son of Prudence by Plato, imitating the holy scriptures of the Hebrews, in which God is called by the same name, so that Dionysius the Areopagite says that Jesus Christ is called the Angel of Prudence and messenger of God, not meaning by Prudence anything but God the First Father. Imitating him later on, Avicenna called the First Cause the advisory cause, which is to show that the Angelic Mind does not have the Ideas and the reasons for things by itself, but from God, and advising someone is nothing but giving him notice and reason for what he has to do. God therefore, having produced the Mind which had to be creator of this visible world, advised it -- taught and instructed it -- in the work it had to do, fashioning that Mind after a most perfect Idea of that artisan of the world.

Chapter Twenty-two

How Love is to be understood as the youngest and oldest of all the gods.

Having explained Diotima's words on the birth of Love and demonstrated that the words of Orpheus, who says that Love was born from the womb of Chaos before all the other gods[1], are compatible with the sense of Plato, it remains for us to show that they are also not opposed to Agathon's statement that Love is younger than all the other gods. This seems obviously to contradict to Orpheus, who makes him older than all the other gods. For an understanding of the true solution one must remember what was said above, that just as a house has two modes of being, one as an idea in the builder's mind and the other in its material, such as stones, timbers, and similar things, and the former is called ideal being and the latter natural being, so it is with all other things which have their ideal being in that First Mind and their natural being outside of it. Jupiter and Saturn and all the other gods can mean both the idea of Saturn and Jupiter and all the other gods and the natural, not the ideal, Saturn and Jupiter.

I say, therefore, that the first god in his natural and perfect being was Love, and before him there was no other god who had natural, perfect being. For all the other gods Love was the cause of the being which is so manifest from the things said above, because Love was born when the Ideas descended into the Angelic Mind. The Ideas being the substance of that Mind, its substance was not perfected until they were perfected, which did not occur until after Love was born. Therefore, if the Angelic Mind did not have its perfect natural being until Love was born, and he was the occasion of giving it that being, then however much by its turning to God those Ideas were made perfect, it can be said all the more of the other gods who came into existence after that Mind that Love existed before they had their perfect natural being, notwithstanding that they came before him in their imperfect ideal being. For this reason he comes to be younger and handsomer than all the

56

other gods, because the Ideas were immediately joined
to that formless nature, and he was not born in it
until after it was already formed by the Ideas,
although imperfectly.

[1]Fr. 169 Kern.

Chapter Twenty-three

How the reign of necessity is understood to have
been prior to that of Love.

On the same basis one can easily understand why
Agathon said that the reign of necessity came before
the reign of Love.[1] To understand this is to
understand why in the Timaeus Plato calls that
formless nature "necessity."[2] Although elsewhere by
necessity he means fate, nevertheless in this place
necessity is to be understood in the first sense, of
arising from that formless nature. Therefore, since
every creature is composed of those two natures,
material and formal, the one imperfect and the other
the cause of perfection, it is to be known that every
time that a creature participates more in the nature
of one it is said to be subject to it, and that one
to predominate over it. For this reason, since the
lower creatures are more imperfect than perfect,
matter is said to predominate in them.

Therefore when the Ideas were still imperfect
and disordered, because that formless and material
nature is the cause of every imperfection, necessity
is said by the theologians then to have reigned.
Because every imperfection which is found in
creatures comes, as is said, from that formless
nature, Agathon says for this reason that all the
things said of the Ideas which denote some
imperfection in them occurred in the reign of
necessity[3], just as all the perfections came after
Love began to rule, because when the Mind is turned
by Love towards God what was formerly imperfect in it
becomes perfect.

[1]Symposium 195a.
[2]47e - 48a.
[3]Symposium loc. cit.

Chapter Twenty-four

Why Venus is said to command the three Fates.

It will not, therefore, be outside our purpose
to explain why Orpheus says that Venus commands all
three of the Fates, which will be clear simply on the
grounds stated above. The Platonists, as we have at
other times said, posit two worlds, this sensible
world and the intelligible world which was the
pattern for this. In this world we see a great deal
of order, and we see everything linked together and
jointly depending in friendly cooperation on the
constitution of a single whole. This order, this
series of causes and effects, the philosophers call
fate, and these earthly things being instances of
Ideas in the intelligible world and depending upon
and subsumed under them, it follows that the order of
the former depends upon the order of the latter, an
order which is called Providence, just as this is
called fate. Therefore the Platonists suppose
Providence, which is the order of the Ideas, to be in
that first Mind. This Providence, this order,
depends on God Himself as the ultimate end of this
order, and the law of Providence, which guides things
towards their end, does not direct them towards
anything but winning that ultimate and infinite good.

Therefore if Venus is nothing but the order of
those Ideas on which depends the earthly order called
fate, it follows that Venus rules over fate, which is
divided into three aspects designated by the names of
the three goddesses, Clotho, Lachesis, and Atropos,
because that order which is united in Providence and
measured in eternity by an indivisible measure, is
divided into three parts, present, past, and future,
although it can also be divided according to the
three kingdoms divided among the sons of Saturn, as
we said in the first book. Some wish to assign
Atropos to the sphere of the fixed stars, Clotho to
the seven planets, and Lachesis to things beneath the
moon.

But to treat of this subject demands its own appointed place. Here it can be understood that nothing is subject to fate but things in time, and these are corporeal. A rational soul, being incorporeal, is therefore not subject to fate but, on the contrary, dominates it,and is subject, rather, to Providence, and serves that whose service is perfect freedom. If our will obeys the law of Providence, it is led most wisely by it in the attainment of its desired end, and every time it wishes to free itself from this service, instead of becoming a free will it becomes a truly servile one, and it makes itself a slave to that fate of which it was formerly the master. Deviating from the law of Providence is nothing but leaving reason and following sense and irrational appetite, which is subject to fate as being of a bodily nature. Whoever is subject to such a will, therefore, makes himself much more the servant of that to which it is a servant. But of this we shall speak another time.

BOOK THREE

Chapter One

<u>Of angelic and human love and their objects.</u>

I believe enough has been said of this heavenly
Love and of Venus, his mother. It is true that if
you wished to pursue all the questions which would
lead to a perfect knowledge of the Ideas it would
need a longer treatise, but in this place it would
be superfluous, and it is our intention to speak
fully of them elsewhere. Leaving this subject for
another time, therefore, and having covered rapidly
what has to be understood about heavenly and angelic
love, we shall pass on to the nature of that love
which is the proper and perfect image of this.

Just as from Uranus, or God, the Ideas descend
into the Angelic Mind and there is born in it the
love of intellectual beauty, so from the Angelic Mind
there descend into the Rational Soul the same Ideas,
which are as much less perfect than those in the
Angelic Mind as the soul and the rational nature are
less perfect than the Angelic Mind and the
intellectual nature, both the nature and name of
which they change, as was said in the first book.

Therefore what was said of Saturn in contrast
with Uranus holds of Jupiter in contrast with Saturn.
Note that Plotinus in his book on love does not speak
of the first, heavenly love but only of this, and so
likewise he does not speak of the first Venus but of
this second one, not of the beauty of the Ideas
descending from Uranus to Saturn, but of that which
descends from Saturn to Jupiter, into the the World-
Soul.¹ He puts this clearly by saying that that
heavenly Venus of whom he speaks was born not of
Uranus, as Plato says, but of Saturn. To one who
does not give careful attention, Plato and Plotinus
would seem to be in disagreement on this matter, but
whoever considers it properly knows the total and
complete knowledge of heavenly love to be different
from that of either of them, because Plato discusses
the first and true heavenly love and Plotinus the
second, which is its image.

Therefore Venus, the mother of this Love, is

born of Saturn and joins with Jupiter, just as that first one is born of Uranus and joins with Saturn, and for the same reason. Just as Plotinus wants the Ideas, which are the first Venus, not to be accidents but the substance of the Angelic Mind, he also wants these particular concepts, which are in the soul as Ideas are in the Mind, to be substantial to the soul. For such a reason as this, Plotinus will now say that the heavenly Venus is that first rational and divine soul. Not to give grounds for error to anyone who is moved by these words to believe that the nature of the soul, in so far as it is rational, is Venus, he adds below that this soul is called Venus in so far as there is in it a certain deceptively splendid love, referring by this to those particular concepts of which we have spoken. Returning to this, I say that just as that first love, which is in the Mind, is called angelic and divine, so this other, which is in the Rational Soul, is called human, because the rational nature is the principal part of man.

Now, having quickly covered what is necessary in regard to heavenly love and its image, we shall pass on to discuss vulgar love, which is nothing but the appetite for the beauty perceived by the sense of sight, as should be clear from the things said above. This beauty, just like the intelligible beauty and absolutely every creature whatever, has three modes of being: causal, formal, and participated. Its cause is the visible heavens, animated by that power which moves them, just as the cause of the intelligible beauty, or Venus, was the first and true intelligible God. This motive power of the heavens is the lowest potentiality of the Heavenly Soul, whereby power is applied to the heavenly bodies just as our motive and impulsive power is to the muscles and nerves which our souls use as organs and instruments to carry out some action. Thus the motive power of the soul of the heavens, which are a body and organ adapted to the everlasting circular heavenly motion just as with animals the feet are adapted to the motion of walking, by means of the heavenly bodies transmutes this inferior matter and endows it with all the forms which are in it, just as the hand of the artist gives his material this or that artificial form with his brush. The cause, therefore, of this earthly Venus, who is the beauty of these material and sensible forms, is that motive power of the Heavenly Soul, and in that this Venus has her causal being.

Her formal and essential being is in the colors
illuminated by the light of the visible sun, just as
the Ideas are by the light of that first, invisible
sun. Her participated being is in the quantitative
arrangement of the beautiful thing, the figure which
consists of such and such an ordering of its parts.
This I call beauty by participation because, as we
have said, beauty is the motivating object of sight,
and since this quantitative arrangement is not
adapted to moving our vision except in so far as it
participates in colors and light, it does not really
have virtue of its own nature but through the
participation and merit of others, who in themselves
and by their own nature are able to move our vision
and generate in the spirit of whoever sees them love
of the thing seen.

[1]Enneads III, v, 203.

Chapter Two

Of heavenly, human, and bestial love, continued.

Vulgar love, is nothing but the desire to
possess such beauty as this and, just as when the
intelligible beauty of the Ideas descended into·the
Angelic Intellect there was forthwith born in the
will of that Intellect a desire to enjoy that beauty
fully, and to win it, this vulgar love is forced to
approach that from which such beauty had come to it,
so as soon as the appearance or image of this
sensible beauty reaches the eye there is suddenly
born in the sensitive appetite, which as we said
above follows sensory cognition just as the will does
the intellectual, so there is born, I say, a desire
to enjoy that beauty fully.

Here there can be born two loves, one of which
is bestial and the other human and rational, because
there is no doubt that to enjoy this beauty fully it
is necessary to unite oneself with the fount and
source from which it proceeds. If we follow the
judgment of the senses, which resembles that of
irrational animals and brutes, we shall judge the

source of this beauty to lie in the material body in which we see it placed, and from this there will arise in us the appetite for coitus, which is nothing but joining oneself to that body in the most intimate way possible.

To discuss this subject at greater length would be to profane Plato's chaste mysteries of love. But let us return to what we intended. I say that the senses judge this beauty to originate from the body, and therefore the goal of love for all the brutes is coitus, but reason judges the exact opposite, knowing not only that that material body is not the source and fount of this beauty but that it is of a nature wholly averse and detrimental to such beauty. It knows that the more it separates itself from the body and considers itself in isolation, the more it has of the proper dignity and excellence of its own nature, and therefore it tries not to resort to the body beyond the appearance received by the eyes, but to purify that appearance as much as it can if it sees any infection of corporeal and material nature left in it.

Because by the word "man" one can understand both the rational soul in its perfect nature and also the rational soul already united and bound to a body, human love in the first sense is just what was said above to be the image of heavenly love. In the other sense this human love of which we were speaking, this love of sensible beauty, is already separated from the body by the soul and made intellectual rather than sensible so far as its nature allows. There are many who rise no higher, and with most men this is what happens. Some more perfect ones remember a more perfect beauty which their souls once saw before they were immersed in bodies, and then there surges up in them an incredible desire to behold it again, and to attain this good they separate themselves from the body as much as they can, so that their souls regain their pristine dignity, completely masters of their bodies and in no way subject to them. Then they are in that kind of love which is the image of heavenly love, and this can be called the perfect kind of human love and the other the fleeting and imperfect kind of human love.

Through this love, if it goes along growing from perfection to perfection, man reaches such a level that his soul is completely united with the Intellect and from a man he becomes an angel, wholly inflamed by this angelic love, as matter kindled by fire and turned to flame rises to the upper part of the lower world. Thus purged of all the dullness of his earthly body and transmuted into spiritual flame by the power of love, soaring even to the intelligible heaven he rests happily in the arms of the Father of all.

Chapter Three

In which souls is found the vulgar love and in which the angelic, and why the heavenly souls are signified by Janus.

From what we have said of the vulgar love, it follows that it can occur only in those souls which are immersed in matter and in some fashion dominated by the body, or at least hampered by it, or in those souls which are not free from emotional disturbances but are subject to their passions. These, according to the Platonists, are our souls and those of the demons, either all of them, as some will have it, or the lower ones closer to our own nature.

Chapter Four

In the other souls, such as ours, it is necessary that there be always that angelic love, just as the intellect of our souls is eternal.[1] Nevertheless, few men display it, the majority, as if with their shoulders turned, having their eyes fixed on sensible things and the care of the body. For a full understanding of this distinction it must be understood that heavenly souls have in them such perfection, as all the Platonists say, that they can perform both functions at the same time, both ruling and administering their bodies yet in so doing not cutting themselves off from the intellectual contemplation of higher things. For the ancient poets these souls were symbolized by the two-faced god Janus because, looking like him both backwards and forwards, they can at the same time see the

intelligible things and see to the sensible. If
other, less perfect souls which do not have eyes
except on one side turn the side on which they have
them towards the body, it is necessary that the other
side be turned towards the intellect, and thus they
are deprived of the vision of intellectual things.
Likewise, if they turn their eyes towards the
intellect they can no longer provide for the body,
and they must give up the care of it. For this
reason those souls which must give up the goods of
the intellect for the care of the body the divine
providence has bound to the care of corruptible and
ephemeral bodies, released from which they can in a
short time, if it is not lacking to them, return to
their intellectual felicity. The other souls, which
are not hindered from the good of the intellect by
care of the body, it has bound to eternal and
incorruptible bodies.

On this basis you can draw the conclusion of an
argument which Aristotle makes in the first book of
De Anima, where he says that if being in the body is
bad for the soul, as Plato often says, it will follow
that the souls of the heavenly bodies are less
fortunate than ours, which will some day be separated
from their bodies. You can also draw another
fundamental principle, that if we suppose all the
demons to be subject to passion we must suppose them
all to be immortal. On this account the definition
given by Apuleius, that the demons are of a nature
capable of suffering but eternal, ought to be
understood as asserting not that there does not occur
in them separation of soul from body, as occurs even
in us, but that they are immortal because their souls
are immortal.

Returning therefore to what we intended, I say
that the heavenly souls, which are symbolized for the
poets by Janus, like those which by means of their
motion are the basis of time, both have eyes to look
at that ideal beauty in the Intellect, which they
continuously love, and have other eyes to look at
lower, sensible things, not to love them or desire
their beauty, but to communicate and give it to them.
Before they are bound to our bodies, our souls are
two-faced in the same way as those because, as Plato
says in the Phaedrus, every soul, meaning every soul
constituted as rational in its nature, is concerned
with the whole physical universe.[1] Even our own

souls, therefore, before they fall into these earthly
bodies, likewise have two faces, in that they can at
the same time both think about intellectual things
and provide for sensible ones. When they descend into
bodies, however, it is as if they were divided down
the middle and of the two faces there remained to
each of them only one, so that every time they turn
these single faces that are left to them towards
sensible beauty they are deprived of the vision of
the other, and so it arises that no one can have both
the vulgar love and the heavenly together. On this
account Zoroaster, encouraging that vision of the
celestial beauty, cries, "Open wide your eyes and
lift them up!"

Good evidence for this is the fact that many
have had their physical eyes, with which sensible
beauty is seen, blinded by the same cause which bore
them off to the vision of intellectual beauty. This
is signified by the fable of Teiresias, chanted by
Callimachus,[2] who for having seen Pallas naked, which
simply means seeing not clothed or covered by matter
that ideal beauty from which comes all genuine
wisdom, became suddenly blind and by the same Pallas
was made a prophet, so that what closed his physical
eyes opened the eyes of his intellect, with which he
was able to see future things no less than present
ones. Homer also was physically blinded, by the shade
of Achilles, by which he was inspired with that
poetic fire which contains in itself all intellectual
contemplation. The apostle Paul was not caught up to
the third heaven until his eyes were made blind to
sensible things by a vision of the divine.[3] Of this
rapture perhaps we shall some time speak.

Returning therefore to the principal subject, I
will say that while our souls are concerned with
sensible things they cannot enjoy the vision of
intellectual beauty. However much that heavenly love
may live in each soul's intellect, nevertheless only
those practice it, and they are few, who are
completely divorced from concern for the body. These
can speak like Paul of not knowing whether they were
in the body or out of it[4], a state to which, like
those whom we call ecstatics, a man sometimes comes
but in which he only briefly lingers. Of the causes
of this separation there are many things to say,
which we shall say at length in our commentary on
Plato's Symposium, because there has not yet been

enough said by others whom I have read.

There will therefore be in us an eternal and substantial love, one which is in the intellect and is angelic, not human. Then, in our souls, which are by nature free and can turn both to sensible beauty and to the intelligible, there can be born three kinds of love, because they love either the sensible beauty or that other, heavenly beauty. If the sensible, they may desire to unite themselves to it bodily, and this desire, because it is based on the irrational judgment that that beauty is derived from that body where it is placed, is the bestial and irrational kind of love. On the other hand, they may desire to unite themselves with it in their minds, perceiving in themselves the appearance and image of that beauty and with continual thought and fixed intention of spirit uniting it to themselves and themselves to it as much as they can. This love, because it is based on rational judgment, on knowing that that beauty not only does not originate in that material body, but on the contrary, by being involved with it, loses the perfection and worth which it recovers when by the power of the soul it is separated from matter, is called human and rational love. The majority of men are wrapped up in these two kinds of love.

Those, however, whose intellects, when purified and illuminated by philosophical study, know that this sensible beauty is an image of another more perfect, begin after giving up this love to see that heavenly beauty. This is that third kind of love which in some degree already tastes that heavenly beauty, having already some memory of it. If such persons persevere in such elevation of mind, they will finally achieve that angelic and intellectual love which, although it was in them first, they nevertheless, occupied with other things, no longer perceived. Of these it can properly be said that the light shone in the shadows and the shadows did not understand it. Of this occurrence we shall speak freely in the exposition of the sixth stanza of the present poem, to the account of which we shall now proceed, after first of all reminding our readers that the fable of Aristophanes related in Plato's Symposium[5], can shed some light on a remark of ours in the second chapter of this treatise. Because nothing pertinent to that is touched upon by our

Poet, however, it is not our duty to interpret it at present.

[1] I have emended Pico's actual words here by inserting this term to accord with the sense of the passage as a whole.

[2] Hymn 5, the third century B.C. Alexandrian poet's account of the Theban seer.

[3] II Corinthians 12:2

[4] II Corinthians 12:3.

[5] 189c - 193d.

TEXTUAL COMMENT

First Stanza

To treat of the two loves belongs to different sciences. Natural and moral philosophers treat of the vulgar love. Theological and, to speak in the fashion of the Peripatetics, metaphysical philosophers treat of the divine. Solomon spoke excellently of both, of the vulgar like a natural philosopher in Ecclesiastes and like a moral philosopher in Proverbs, and of the divine and heavenly love in his Canticles,[2] and on that account the Hebrews Johanan[1] and Manaen[2] and the Chaldean Jonathan[3] say that of all the hymns of holy scripture it is the holiest and most divine. Two poets have specifically treated in the Tuscan tongue of these two loves, Guido Cavalcanti of the vulgar in one of his songs, and our own Poet of the other in the present work, in which, however much he may deal with both, he nevertheless treats principally of the heavenly and does not speak of the former except in so far as it is a feeble image of the latter.

Within his hands Love holds the reins. . .

and after many lines he adds

Love puts my tongue and talent under
strain. . . .

This is the beginning of the present poem; the other, composed by Guido, begins

A lady prays that I should choose to speak[4]

and it is said by his expounders that by that lady is to be understood Love. In these openings are to be noted three differences.

The first is that Guido says that love prays him, and our Poet says that Love puts him under strain. The second is that love is here called by its own name, which Guido doesn't choose to do. The third is that the latter represents it as a woman and the former does not, but by the customary name of "love", which by its pronunciation is a masculine noun. These differences do not arise from any mistake

71

by either of the poets nor from divergent opinions, but because each speaks appropriately of the love which is the topic of his poem.

I said in the preceding paragraph that Guido treated of the vulgar love and our Poet of the heavenly. A rational soul should not be subjected to the vulgar love but should rather dominate over it, because it is located among the inferior, sensory appetites, subordinate to the irrational part of the soul. For that reason Guido says that love <u>prays</u> him, not <u>puts him under strain</u>, showing that the sensory appetites can do no violence to reason, though many, to excuse their vices, say that the counsel of human reason cannot resist the attacks of the sensitive part, though this can only pray reason, that is, invite it and entice it to its wishes, to which reason can condescend and consent without blame when they are moderate, but by which it can in no way be compelled. This is the contrary of the heavenly love, to which, placed in the intellectual part, as stated in my second book, it ought deservedly to be subordinate, since it is inferior. The inferior nature does not retain its freedom except when it is the handmaiden of the superior. On that account our Poet fittingly subjects himself to the force of the heavenly love, recognizing in it his greatest liberty.

The reason for the second difference, Guido's not calling love by its proper name, is that the vulgar love is not true love at all, just as sensible beauty is not true beauty but its image. So the vulgar love is but a semblance and shadow of the heavenly, which alone claims as its own the most holy name of love, nor is the name suitable in any fashion to the other except as it is the custom to call the statue of Hercules <u>Hercules</u> and the face of Helen, whether painted or sculptured, <u>Helen</u>.

The reason for the third difference, Guido's use of a feminine noun to signify love and our Poet's of a masculine one, is that the vulgar love bears to the heavenly the same proportion as an imperfect thing to a perfect, and by the Pythagoreans the imperfect nature was signified by the feminine and the perfect by the masculine; nor shall I refrain from adding to this that the vulgar love, which is of physical beauty, is more fittingly a love for women than for

men. The heavenly is the opposite, as Plato wrote in
the speech of Pausanias in the <u>Symposium</u>[5]. The
vulgar, being a passion of the sensitive soul, comes
close to letting us rush headlong into the union of
coitus, since it pertains to that part of the soul
more irrational than rational. When, overcome by
weakness, one falls into this act, it is less
unsuitable for the female sex than for the other.

The opposite is the heavenly love, in which this
danger does not arise, but everything is directed
towards the spiritual beauty of the mind and
intellect, which are much more perfect in men than in
women, as is seen with every other perfection. On
this account all those who have been kindled by this
divine love have for the most part loved young men of
noble character whose virtues have been as pleasing
to others as the bodies in which they reside are
handsome. They have not made themselves effeminate
like a pack of prostitutes who not only do not bring
men to any degree of spiritual perfection but, like
Circe, transform them into utter beasts. With this
chaste love Socrates loved not only Alcibiades but
almost all the most clever and graceful young men of
Athens. So Zeno was loved by Parmenides, Musaeus by
Orpheus, Nicomachus by Theophrastus, and Cleinias by
Xenophon. None of these wished to carry on any foul
practices with their loved ones but only, through
arousing themselves by their external and physical
beauty, to behold that of their souls, from which
emanated and came that physical beauty and, the
beauty of the soul being a participation in the
angelic beauty, to raise themselves, surging ever
higher, to a more sublime degree of contemplation in
order to arrive at the primary source of all beauty,
God. This is the fruit which Plato sought from his
love and not that shameful sort which Dicearchus[6]
imputes to him. This Socrates often achieved when,
many times, inspired by the beauty of Phaedrus, he
sang of the highest mysteries of theology by the
river Ilissus.

<u>Within his hands Love holds the reins</u>. . . .
Among the other rules imposed on created things by
divine wisdom is seen this in particular: that every
lower nature is governed by that immediately superior
to it, and so long as it obeys the higher one, the
lower, protected from every evil, is led to its
appointed felicity without impediment, and if, from

too much love of its own liberty and preference for a
licentious life rather than a more useful one, it
rebels against obedience to the higher nature, like a
small boy against the yoke of the master, it incurs a
double penalty. The first is that, like a ship
abandoned by the pilot, it strikes now on this rock,
now on that, without hope of making port. The other
is that it loses its power over other natures
subordinate to it just as it has rebelled against
that higher one, a fact which, to make more manifest,
we shall explain with examples drawn by theologians
from the holy mysteries. An irrational nature is
governed by the foresight of others, and because of
its imperfection it is not adapted to the guidance of
any other creatures, just as God through his
ineffable excellence provides for all beings and has
no need for the providence of any other. Between God
and the lower animals as the two extremes are the
angels and rational souls, which are governed by
others and have others governed by them. The highest
angels, immediately enlightened and instructed, as it
were, by God, instruct and advise the lower angels,
as one reads in the prophet Daniel and as is more
particularly explained by Dionysius the Areopagite.
The last order of angels immediately above us, called
demoni by the Platonists and Pythagoreans and Issim
by the Hebrews, a name derived from Is, which means
man, is assigned to our governance like guards and
shepherds of men, just as we are to the governance of
all irrational nature. On that David says rightly
that men are but little lower than the angels and
that under their feet are placed the cattle, the
fish, the birds, and all the brute beasts.[7] By these
words it is also to be observed that the beasts are
much more distant from our perfection than we are
from the angels'. The brutes are under our feet and
we are but little diminished from the dignity of the
angels.

Therefore, so long as the highest angels subject
themselves to the yoke of divine power they retain
their own dignity and their rule and authority over
other creatures. When through unmeasured love of
their own excellence, however, they aspire to such
equality with God that they wish to preserve
themselves like Him without any aid but their own
strength (into which error, through the gift of grace
in which they are established, they cannot now fall
but into which Lucifer and his followers once fell,

as both our own theologians and the ancient cabalists tell us), then they are hurled from their blessedness into the abyss of extreme misery, and every power over other creatures is taken from them as it was from Lucifer, who now, seeing us freed from his dominion, enviously lays constant traps for our welfare. Likewise, as long as Adam placed himself in obedience to his superiors and did not rebel against the divine precepts and counsels he was most happy, and lord of all the animals. He lost both when, through eagerness to rival God Himself in the knowledge of good and evil and by this means, as it were, to free himself from His governance as though no longer needing it, he deviated from the divine commandment by tasting the forbidden fruit.

This same order is seen in the little world of our souls, in which the lower powers are instructed and corrected by the higher and, while they trust them, carry on their work without error. The imagination often corrects the mistakes of the outer senses. Reason administers the imagination and is illuminated by the intellect. It never falls into error except when either the imagination impudently withholds its faith from it or it trusts too much in its own strength in opposition to the intellect. Likewise, among the appetites, the sensory is governed by the rational and the rational by the intellectual. Our Poet has subtly touched on this in speaking of the reins of his heart as held by hands of love.

In the second book we declared the heavenly love to be the intellectual appetite. In every well-organized soul every other appetite ought on this account to be governed by it, a governance which is denoted by the reins, imitating the language of the Phaedrus.[8] Therefore the Poet speaks of his heart as being guided by love, each of his desires depending on that one, and he says "heart" because, as is observed in both the philosophers and the holy scriptures, the activity of the cognitive powers of the soul is commonly attributed to the head and of the appetitive ones to the heart.

And in his sanctified domain. . . . A man who looks for some new benefit from others cannot attract it to himself by any better means than by that sort

75

of liberality which shows itself grateful for
benefits already received. On that account our Poet,
looking for help from love in his present enterprise,
demonstrates a most grateful disposition, because the
"flame of love", by which his talent has been
uplifted to the highest intellectual beauty, refers
neither to the source of, nor to any increase in,
either his merits or his powers but, by his humbly
calling himself unworthy of it, shows itself to be
both born and nourished in him by the kindness of
love.

My heart is terrified. . . . Having shown how by
the power and command of love he has been led to this
enterprise, in the rest of this first stanza he says
two things: that by his own strength he cannot hope
to be able to bear such a burden and that with the
help of love he hopes for every result desired.

My tongue. . . . The same lack of ability which
makes the tongue an unsuitable agent for such a task
also makes it powerless to resist and oppose the
greater strength of that which moves it to speak.

> . . . has pledged
> those wings. . . .

Here the Poet touches on a solemn doctrine of
theologians and metaphysicians that every time some
higher virtue is said to descend into us it is not to
be understood that by descending from its own sublime
station it puts itself into a lower place to join
itself to us but rather that by its own power it
draws us to itself. Its descent into us is a
compulsion upon us to ascend to it, because otherwise
there would result from such a conjunction only an
imperfection for that virtue rather than perfection
for the one who receives it. What deceives the common
imagination is the idea that the conjunction of
spiritual things is like that of physical ones, which
are conjoined through proximity in site and place.
Thus people believe that the intellectual light
cannot join our souls unless, like an inhabitant of a
higher place, it comes down from heaven to earth, as
it were, to couple itself to us. The Poet indicates
this by telling us that the same wings on which love
descends are those with which he himself is to be
elevated to the sublime contemplation of the
mysteries of love.

Embellishing its crest. . . . Here the poet
shows two things: first, that this love under whose
lordship he has lived and lives is the heavenly love
and not the vulgar, saying that love left its plumes
at the top of his breast, meaning by this with the
higher powers of his immortal soul -- the lower,
which are the sensitive ones, being the lodging of
the vulgar love. The other is that since love has
already dwelt in him a long time and made a nest in
his heart, he is able to speak of it truly and
devotedly, as a thing well-known and familiar to him.

[1]Probably Johanan ben Zakkai, first century
Palestinian rabbi.
[2] Menachem de Recanati, an early 14th century
Italian Jewish cabalist.
[3]Probably the third century rabbi Jonathan ben
Eleazar, who was born in Babylonia, or possibly
Jonathan ben Uzziel, who translated some of the
prophets into Aramaic. Cf. Note 1, pg. 29.
[4]This is the poem Donna mi priega.
[5]180c ff.
[6]Sicilian Peripatetic philosopher and pupil of
Aristotlte, fl. c. 320 B.C.
[7]Psalms 8:5.
[8]246a ff.

Second Stanza

I shall tell[1] how love. . . .

In this stanza the author does two things:
first, he briefly sets forth what he has to say about
love; then, as though moved by the celebration he has
just made of the greatness of the subject of which he
proposes to treat, he turns to invocation, calling
Apollo to his aid along with Love. He says in the
first part that he will tell how

. . . . Love from the fountainhead divine
Of uncreated good. . . .

77

-- that is, of divine beauty, the primal source, as has been stated, of all beauty and consequently of love, which is born of it -- <u>descends down here</u>, into our souls, in which its effect <u>ultimately</u> terminates.

He will also tell, as he does in the following stanza, <u>when and how it was first born</u>, in the Angelic Mind on the birthday of Venus, that is, of ideal beauty. In the second book three principal things were said of this: first, that the order of those Ideas which we try to denote by <u>Venus</u> is the order of the providence by which this <u>lower</u> world is ruled and governed; second, that that ideal splendor, by the generous sharing of the Angelic Mind, is communicated to the Rational Soul, by the loving revolutions of which the heavenly bodies are ultimately moved by the perfect Mind. Of these three things the Poet promises to speak, saying below that he will tell how Love

> . . . moves and shapes all souls and rules the world.

He begins with the motion of the heavens, which is the final effect, and ascends in sequence from that to the first, which is the ruling of the world by the righteous regime of providence. In setting forth the promised account he takes the reverse order, to show that although in the search for a truth of which a dim light and confused awareness appear to our minds it may be a useful and necessary order, as Aristotle declares, to proceed from lower things, which are nearer and more familiar to us, to higher ones, nevertheless, after the truth has been found, whoever has to speak of it scientifically and, as Plato everywhere observes, divinely, ought in his writing to keep the natural order of the things themselves, that is, as lower things emanate and come forth from higher ones, so in scientific order one descends from knowledge of the latter to knowledge of the former.

Of these three effects the Poet speaks continually through the whole poem as the context demands. It is to be understood that love is not the efficient cause of these effects, because love is not what produces the Ideas in the Angelic Mind, for this is God, nor what makes the Soul shine with the

78

splendor of the Ideas, for this is the Mind, nor what moves the heavens, for they have no other movers than their own souls. Rather, love is the cause of these things because without it the effects would not follow from their principal causes. If the Mind did not turn to God and the Soul to the Mind, of which turning the cause is Love, the Ideas would not descend into the former nor particular concepts into the latter. If the Soul were not perfected and illuminated by these, it would not be a suitable agent for drawing these sensible forms from the bosom of lower matter by the motion of the heavens.

Therefore the Poet will declare how love is the cause of these effects; then finally he will tell how men are compelled by the power of heavenly love to raise themselves from earth, from sensible things, to heaven, to sublime and spiritual things. He will tell by what law and in what fashion there lives in us now that heavenly love which turns us towards heaven, and now that vulgar love which turns us towards earth and now puts us in a middle state between these two extremes, both as he will suggest in the final stanza and as we stated at length in the preceding book. Under the heavenly love are understood the fifth and sixth grades of love, and under the vulgar the first, second, and third, and by the middle state is meant the fourth grade, of which it is not necessary to speak here since at the beginning of stanzas V, VI, and VII, in which the Poet speaks of it, we shall treat of it at more length.

As for the second part of the stanza, only one doubtful point remains to be brought out, the reason for which the Poet has called both Love and Apollo to his aid. For this it should be known that for everyone who has to speak on some topic two things are necessary: first, an adequate concept of its nature, and second, the ability to explain his conception in an agreeable and elegant style, whether in writing or in discourse.

To achieve the first it is necessary not only to have in one's mind a good knowledge of that thing but to transform oneself wholly into it. No one will never treat well of a sad topic who does not first clothe himself in sadness within his own mind, and whoever has to write of a martial event, like a war,

not only needs a simple knowledge of it but also,
wishing to portray and express it in his speech,
needs first to bring himself into a similar condition
internally, and so with every other subject. On this
account whoever has to speak of love must transform
himself into love. What can transform water into
fire except fire? What can transform us into love
except love?   Its aid is therefore necessary to
whoever would write of it, since one cannot write of
it who does not become love.

In achieving the second thing we need the help
of whoever can give us the gift of eloquence, which
was attributed by the ancients to the Muses and
Apollo. For this reason, therefore, Apollo and Love
are invoked by our Poet, just as in addition to the
gods who give eloquence, Mars is invoked by those who
write of wars and Hymen by those who write of
weddings, as we shall state in somewhat more detail
in the first book of our Poetic Theology.

This is enough for the present explanation; and
it is not without reason that the invocation to Love
was made only once and that to Apollo was made with
an agreeable repetition[2], joining it to that to Love.
The true and perfect understanding of a thing without
speaking or writing of it can well be conceived, but
one cannot speak or write of it well who does not
first conceive or understand it. On this account
Love's help and kindness to us cannot come by
themselves but must bring with them the help of
Apollo. Neither can the help of Apollo occur in any
fashion without that of Love. As conceiving a thing
comes before explaining it, so the invocation to Love
ought properly, as our Poet has made it in the first
stanza, to come before that to Apollo, which he now
makes in the second.

[1]Pico makes this verb future. In Benivieni it
is present.
[2]Since Apollo seems mentioned or referred to
only once in this stanza, it is difficult to see just
what repetition Pico is alluding to, unless he is
confusing an invocation to Apollo with that to Love
to which he refers at the end of this paragraph.

Third Stanza

<u>Reflected from the one true heaven.</u> . . .

        In this third stanza our Poet tells us very
elegantly where Love was first born and how, and
finally what love is. Because we discussed all this
material at length in the second book, a simple
explanation of the words will be enough here. In
summary, the meaning of the whole stanza is this:
that when from God there descends into the Angelic
Mind, <u>its firstling</u>, the first of God's creatures, an
ample supply of Ideas, that Mind, desiring them in
their perfection, turns to God and obtains from Him
full possession of what it desires, which it loves
the more ardently the more fully it has it in itself.
Finally the Poet concludes that that desire, which is
born both of the Mind, in so far as it is not yet
illumined, and of the Ideas received into it, is the
love of which he speaks in the present stanza.

        He says, therefore,

        Reflected from the one true heaven. . .

that is, from God as first among all things, as the
heavens are first among all corporeal things. He
says "true" because intelligible and spiritual things
are held by the Pythagoreans and all ancient
theologians to be the only true ones, and sensible
beings their images and shadows, differing from them
almost as an alchemist's gold, which is made by art,
differs from true and natural gold. And because
between the philosopher and the sophist there is the
same difference, that the philosopher seeks the true
and the sophist the apparent, the ancient Platonists
say that the maker of sensible things is called a
sophist. Not to give anyone grounds for error,
however, it is to be noted that God is called the
true and intelligible heaven, like that which is the
Idea for this sensible one, not because the Ideas are
produced in the first Mind by God, as stated in the
first book, but rather by way of likeness and
translation because, just as heaven, which is one
part of the highest world, contains and preserves all
other earthly things in itself, so God encloses and

81

preserves every created thing in the infinite compass
of His indivisible and utterly simple unity.

Celestial light. . . descends refers to the
light of the Ideas emanating from God, the source of
all spiritual light just as in the heavens the sun is
of all sensible light. The sun is said to descend
where its light and its power descend. Into the
great Angelic Mind: mind and intellect are that very
thing which it, namely the sun, tends and nourishes
because, as stated above, those Ideas are the
substantial form of the Angelic Mind; on that account
it was not enough to say tends, which indicates only
accidental perfection. Its firstling, that is, the
Angelic Mind as the first of God's creatures, beneath
the living leaves, that is, under the adornment of
the Ideas, which by the Poet's use of the word leaf
is made clear to anyone who remembers that in Chapter
XIV[1] of the second book it was said that the formless
essence of the angels is signified for Plato by the
Gardens of Jupiter, in which the Ideas are planted by
God like ever-verdant and leafy trees. He says
"living" because a thing is called living which has
within itself an intrinsic principle for carrying out
its own function, which is in a broad sense called
self-motion. From this it follows that the Angelic
Mind, having by means of those Ideas an inner
principle in itself suitable for performing its
function, which is to understand, can properly be
said to have life as they do, a life surely worthy
and noble, of which David says to God "Give me
understanding and I shall live"[2], thinking whoever
exists without it to be more dead than alive and
whoever shares in it to live a perfect life, lovable
and eternal, which the contemplative philosophers
enjoy as much as is possible in this world. Our
author also applies the epithet of life to the Ideas
in order to follow John the Evangelist, who, wishing
to show what was created by God to have been in Him
first of all in its ideal being, said "and all the
things made in Him were life".[3] The secret mysteries
of the cabalists agree with this, which attribute the
term life to the second sefiroth, that is, numbering,
which proceeds from the First Father and is in itself
the first ideal wisdom.

Its primal blessing. . . .

The light illuminates and warms, but first it illuminates and then it warms, and since it has warmed more than at first it perfectly illuminated, whoever receives it, since he is inflamed by the heat, becomes more like the nature of light, more adapted to being formed by it. Thus the light of the Ideas, descending into the Angelic Mind first illuminates it, though not perfectly, but since from such a light there is born in it the heat of a most ardent desire and inextinguishable thirst to satisfy itself at the source of that light, borne by such ardor as in a chariot of fire it reaches the place where, by the infinite generosity of the First Father, that God in whom no envy lodges, as much of the desired light overflows into it as it is able to receive, like sweetest nectar. Because the more it drinks of this, the more it wants, and the more it tastes its sweetness, the Poet adds:

And now that first desire. . . .

that is, to possess ideal beauty completely. This desire, this love, transforms the loving mind into the thing loved. Such a desire as this, I say, when it receives more of the divine splendor into itself for greater approximation to <u>uncreated radiance's Sun</u>, which is God,

Miraculously kindles

through innate desire. Perhaps someone might ask why he says "innate", when that desire is born in it from the Ideas it has received, which it does not possess by itself but which come into it from outside, from the First Father. I would give the reply that although it receives these Ideas, the origin of this desire, from elsewhere, nevertheless it does not receive them as accidental things distinct from its own substance but as its first intrinsic and substantial function, and to show this the Poet, believing these Ideas to come down into the Angelic Mind as distinct and exterior to its own substance, calls this ardor innate, that is, inborn, a natural and not an accidental desire.

That heat, that flame, that burning

What the poet adds here has been adequately stated in the second book, that the desire to possess

83

ideal beauty, which was born both from the Angelic
Mind, dark in itself, and from the first perfect
light reflected into it, is the first love there can
be in the world and the truest, just as the beauty
loved by it is the truest that may be thought of.
And it is in the same words clearly told how this
love is born of wealth and poverty, which are called
Porus and Penia by Plato, and likewise how it is born
when Venus, who is honored in Cyprus, is brought
forth by Uranus. Not without reason has the Poet
chosen here with poetic grace to refer to Porus and
Penia both by feminine names, wealth and poverty[4],
rather than following strictly the words of Plato
and representing the one by a masculine name, the
other by a feminine.   He has done this because
wealth and poverty, the possession in some fashion of
the beloved object and in some fashion one's
deprivation of it, are not the principal and
efficient cause of love, which we said above would be
its father, but come under that sort of cause spoken
of by the philosophers without which the effect does
not follow. Because the Platonists say that this
reduces to the nature of a material cause, as being
less important and less worthy, the Poet therefore
translated both by feminine words.

[1]Actually XIII.
[2]Psalms 119:144
[3]1:4.
[4]Richezza and inopia in Italian.

Fourth Stanza

Because . . . that god. . . .

The perfect knowledge of anything consists in
the understanding both of its particular nature and
of all the properties which follow from that nature.
Sometimes through the properties known to us we
investigate the nature of the thing, and sometimes,
by an opposite process, from a knowledge of the
nature itself one arrives at an understanding of the
properties, and this method, which is a great deal
better, our Poet has followed here, having stated the
nature of love in the third stanza, deriving from
that in the present one its principal property and

84

then assigning the reason for the noblest effects which love works in us.

Because. . . that god . . . . This assigns the first property with its reason, and since this is the first and true love, on which every other love depends, born of ideal beauty, which is called the Cyprian, or Venus, for the above reason every love and beauty must direct itself towards these, and on that account no desire for anything deformed or shameful can claim for itself the most sacred name of love.

Therefore our first[1]desire. . . . The second effect of love is this: that there is excited in us by it the yearning for that heavenly and intelligible beauty, every desire for which, the soul having been oppressed by the body and forgotten, remains lulled and put to sleep, but aroused anew by love it is awakened and, following an honored trail from the sensible beauty of bodies to that of the soul and thence to the Angelic Mind, ultimately leads to the bosom of divinity itself, the first fount of all beauty.

By Love the fire. . . . Wonderful and secret mysteries of love are contained in the next five lines, especially when he says that in us is kindled the fire of love in which the heart burns while dying and burning in that death nevertheless grows. Surely he conceals in a few words a very deep sense, which is this: that the more effectively our soul is engaged in the exercise of one of its potentialities or powers, the weaker its other activities are left, and that when everything is directed towards one, the others, except those of which merely animal life consists, are left deficient in everything. This will be clearer in an example: if someone is deeply engaged in daydreaming, the operation of the external senses fails, as in the experience of those who, while fixed in deep thought of something, neither hear someone speaking to them nor see what is placed before their eyes. Thus whoever is wholly withdrawn into the rational part of himself thinks and sees with the pure eye of reason without any activity of the imagination accompanying it. Likewise, whoever arrives at the exercise of the intellectual part will lack the acts and operations of both reason and all other lower cognitive powers.

85

And because, as said in the first book, the
rational part is peculiar to man and through the
intellectual he communicates with the angels, this
latter lives a life no more human than angelic and,
dead to tne sensible world, is reborn to a more
perfect life in the intellectual. Motion and
activity are the signs of life. The lack of these is
the sign of death. Therefore when no human activity
is apparent in a man he is truly dead to human
existence, and if from that he passes to an
intellectual mode of being, by such a death he is
transformed from man to angel. In no other way
should the saying of the wise cabalists be understood
when they say that Enoch was transformed into
Metatron, an angel of God³ or any other man into an
angel. And on this account, if the divine and
heavenly love of which the author speaks is
intellectual desire, as was stated in the second
book, and one cannot pass over to such a mode of
being unless he first dies as far as the human part
of the soul is concerned, the Poet properly says that
while the heart, or the human soul which dwells in
the heart, burns with the fire of love it dies in
that fierce heat, but in that dying it suffers no
failure but rather grows, because consumed by that
fire like the holiest holocaust, sacrificed to the
First Father, the fount of beauty, it is happily
conducted by ineffable grace to the temple of Solomon
adorned with all spiritual richness, a true dwelling
place of divinity. This is the inestimable gift of
love which makes men equal to angels, an admirable
faculty which through death gives one life.

From this you can understand the deep reason for
which Plato put into the speech of Phaedrus in the
Symposium the tales of Alcestis and Orpheus, which we
shall see conforming to our exposition above only in
an anagogical sense, in which both the thought of
Plato and the profundity of this subject are
perfectly stated. It is thus the intention of Plato
to show that there is no hope of being able to reach
the fruition of intellectual beauty by any route
unless, first completely abandoning the lower
potentialities, one abandons human life with them.
Neither does one love perfectly, with perfect love,
who does not die from love. I say "with perfect
love" because that love which in the second book we
said to be the image of heavenly love can lodge in

one who is still human, although it resides in the
rational part, but with that love which is pure and
truly intellectual, the antiquity and dignity of
which is there expounded by Phaedrus, none can clothe
himself who does not first divest himself of this
life, separating not the body from the soul but the
soul from the body.

Alcestis loved perfectly, therefore, choosing to
go to her beloved through death, and dying for love
she was restored to life by the grace of the gods,
brought back to life not by physical but by spiritual
regeneration. But he errs greatly who, not plucking
himself entirely away from the sensible world but
still living in it, believes that he can be united to
the perfect ideal sublimity which is the object of
our love, because the Ideas themselves, in their true
being, cannot be seen except with the eye of
intellectual virtue, which does not undergo
association with the activity of the lower virtues
but constantly excites, burns up, consumes, and like
the liveliest fire converts into itself whoever
approaches it. In tne other lower potentialities,
whether rational or imaginative, the Ideas are not
seen in themselves but only in their images or
likenesses, more perfect in the reason which the
Peripatetics call the passive intellect than in the
fantasy or imagination just as the former is closer
to the true intellect. Plato couldn't say this more
gracefully or subtly than by the example he uses of
Orpheus, of whom he says that when he wished to go to
see his beloved Eurydice he would not condescend to
die to go to her but, as if made soft and effeminate
by his music, sought only to go to her while still
living, and therefore Plato says that he could not
win the real Eurydice, but only a shadow or phantasm
of her was shown to him.

It happens in the same way with any who, not
plucking themselves away from the activities of the
imaginative part and even of the rational, hope to
arrive at a true knowledge of the intellectual Ideas,
because they see these not in themselves and in their
true being but only phantasms or likenesses of them,
either in the passive intellect or in the glistening
imagination. Although this notion is subtle and
deep, it is nevertheless so much in conformity with
things that it seems to me a marvel that neither
Marsilio nor anyone else, taken in by the words of

87

Plato, has understood it. My conscience is my
witness that the first time I ever read the
Symposium I had not finished reading his words in
this place before this truth came into my mind, which
I shall explain at more length in my commentary on
the Symposium and in my Poetic Theology. I want to
leave this knot to be untied by whoever reads: that[4]
the same serpent that deprived Orpheus of Eurydice
taught him music and prevented him from regaining his
beloved Eurydice through his own death. I don't want
to open up this secret any further -- he that hath
ears to hear, let him hear.

For a more complete statement of this matter, it
should be further known only that sometimes the soul
is said to be separated from the body but not the
body from it. This occurs when all of the powers of
the soul, except that which nourishes the body,
called the vegetative, are bound and do nothing, as
if they were simply not. This, as has been said,
happens when the intellectual part, the queen of the
soul, is active, which because of its dignity does
not regard with indulgence the activity of any other
power except the nutritive, whose functions, because
of their great distance from it, are not nullified,
although greatly weakened. But if the intellectual
activity is strengthened and prolonged, the soul must
separate itself even from this last, vegetative part
in such a way that both it is separated from the body
and the body from it.

Therefore by the first death, which is the
separation only of the soul from the body and not the
opposite, the lover can see the beloved heavenly
Venus, and, face to face with her, thinking of her
divine image, happily feast his purified eyes. But
whoever wishes to possess her still more intimately
and, not content with seeing and hearing her, be
deemed worthy of her intimate embraces and panting
kisses must totally separate himself from the body by
the second death, and then he not only sees and hears
the heavenly Venus but clasps her to himself in an
indissoluble knot, and, tranfusing their souls into
each other with kisses, the more they change the more
they are united together so perfectly that each of
their two souls, and both, can be called one single
soul. And notice that the most perfect and intimate
union which the lover can have with his heavenly
beloved is denoted by the union of a kiss, because no

other encounter or coupling more common in corporeal love is it in any way lawful to use as a symbol for this holy and most sacred love.

Because the wise cabalists believe many of the ancient patriarchs to have died in such a state of intellectual rapture, you will find them said to have died of binsica, which in our language means death from a kiss, which they attribute to Abraham, Isaac, Jacob, Moses, Aaron, Mary, and some others. Whoever does not understand our basis for this will never fully understand their meaning. You will read nothing more in their books except that binsica, death from a kiss, occurs when the soul so unites itself in intellectual rapture to things separate from it that, uplifted from the body, it abandons it completely. Why for such a death such a name is appropriate has not, so far as I have read, been hitherto explained by others. This is what the divine Solomon is wishing for when he cries out in his Canticles, "Kiss me with the kisses of your mouth".⁵ In this verse Solomon shows the whole intention of the book and the final aim of his love. Plato means this by the kisses of his Agathon and not what many, seeing themselves in Plato, believe of him. You will never see Solomon or Plato, or anyone else who has spoken of the heavenly love, going beyond a kiss.

> For whom by Love what lives in him's begun,
> In him by Love the fire is lit, and lo --
> The heart in dying burns, and burning, grows.

We have stated how, burning in the fire of love, the heart dies and by such a death rises to a more sublime life. The statement of the other part, how by means of this fire of love there comes to others what lives in it, we shall give fully in the exposition of the next text.

For him the deathless fountain. . . . By the deathless fountain he means God, and it is a name attributed to Him by the ancient cabalists also, and if there were no love there would not descend from this fountain the inestimable supply of those living waters which rain down first into the Angelic Mind and are then, still through love, received into the Soul, by which, through the motion of the heavens, is produced that which is generated anew in the sensible

89

world around us.   The Angelic Mind would not receive
the influx of divine goodness if it did not direct
itself towards it, nor is it directed except by love,
as we have said, nor would the Soul participate in
the Angelic light if it were not likewise directed
towards it by loving desire.   Therefore love is the
cause for the production of everything which proceeds
from God, understanding by love what Plato and our
Poet understand, not love which might be in Him, as
Marsilio believes, because then there would be
imperfection in Him, but the love of his creatures
for Him, as we have stated and in our fashion said.

   What lives in him's begun in him.   .   .   .   that
is, what lives in the Mind.   To declare that this
love is not an accident or quality of that Mind but
pertains to its substance, the Poet says that what is
in the Mind is also in that love by the merit of
which the perfection of the Ideas is in it, and being
then brought into the Soul the production and design
of what is contained in the sensible world arises and
results from it.   For the above reasons the rest of
the stanza is clear and needs no further explanation,
and it was stated in the first and second books what
that eternal love is with which our souls burn
continuously, although when we are frozen in the ice
of matter no feeling of this heat reaches us.   For
this reason we can well bewail our lot with David:
the waters are come in even unto my inmost soul[6], and
blessed is he who can say: the great multitude of the
waters of this my corporeal abyss has not been able
to extinguish in me the fire of divine love.

   [1]I have followed Benivieni's use of the word
primo here.   In this quotation, however, Pico says
pigro[2], or "lazy".
      [3]Cf. III Enoch.
      [3]By its lethal bite.   Cf. Virgil, Georgics iv,
457. [4]
      [4]Canticles 1:2.
      [5]Psalms 69:1.

90

Fifth Stanza

As from the Highest Good. . . .

Here the Poet tells how the vulgar Venus is
born, sensible beauty. As we have treated this topic
adequately in the second book, a simple explanation
of the author's words will be enough for us here.
Therefore, just as the Angelic Mind has its being,
its life, and its understanding from God, so the
Rational Soul, which is produced from that Mind, has
from it its motion, its understanding, and its
imagination. This is because the Rational Soul
understands itself and the other incorporeal things,
moves the eternal corporeal ones -- the heavenly
spheres -- and manufactures and shapes corruptible
corporeal ones by the motion of the eternal bodies,
because by moving them, as the author suggests, it
impresses on lower matter those Forms of things which
it has conceived in itself, by which Forms, like rays
of the intelligible sun, it is illumined. As it
receives them from the Angelic Mind, so it
communicates them to matter. Thus it diffuses what
it contains, producing every particular nature which
is subordinate to it. And because from it, the
rational soul, is produced the sensitive and moving
soul of the body and also the vegetative soul, as is
proved in the Timaeus[1], on this account the Poet adds
that that which then moves, lives, and feels, has all
these functions from it. Therefore from it, the
Moving Soul of the heavens, called Jupiter by Plato
in the Symposium, Venus, the sensible beauty of
bodies, is born here below, in the inferior matter
signified for Plato by Dione, just as from heaven,
God, is born in the Intellect, the Angelic Mind, that
other Venus which is heavenly beauty.

Reflected in the Sun. . . . At the end of
this stanza, in a few words, the author covers the
highest senses of earthly beauty, drawn from the
crumbs of the secret doctrines of ancient
philosophers and theologians. By an understanding of
these it is to be known that since beauty is an
object of sight and everything visible is visible by
means of light, it follows that the actuality, the
Form, and the efficacy of every beauty depends on

91

light, whether physical, if the beauty is physical,
or intelligible or spiritual, if the beauty is
spiritual. Therefore, before the Ideas descended
into the formless essence of the Angelic Mind their
being was like that of colors and visible figures at
night, before the splendor of the sun's rays descends
upon them. One who sees a beautiful body by the
nocturnal light of the moon wants to see it in the
clearer light of day to be able to enjoy that beauty
more fully than is possible in the dim and shadowy
light of the night. In this way, seeing the ideal
beauty in itself, but only dimly and obscurely, and
not being able to see it except feebly in the night
of its own imperfection and in the shadows of its
nature, because, just as the moon does not shine by
itself, the Angelic Mind possesses no perfection by
itself if it does not turn to the First Father, it
wished with loving desire to turn to the paternal Sun
and, clothed in its abundant light, to make its
beauty more perfect, and make its intellectual eye
light up so that it could[2] fully enjoy the beloved
beauty. So it turned,[3] and as it turned God said "Let
light be made"[3], and thereupon light was made,
spiritual and intelligible light, which renders the
face of the heavenly Venus most beautiful in itself
and clearly visible to the eye of the first Mind,
which, thanking the generosity of the Father and
turned towards Him, sings: "Marked above us is the
light of Thy face. With Thee is the fountain of
life; in Thy light shall we see light."[4]

In the same way with physical beauty we have two
things to consider. The first is the sensible
object itself, which so far as its primary substance
is concerned is the same at midnight as at midday.
The other is the light of day which, joining itself
to the object, is to it almost as the soul to the
body. Having presupposed this, our Poet imagines
that as the first part of sensible beauty proceeds
from the first part of intellectual beauty, corporeal
forms from the ideal Forms, so this sensible light
may proceed and emanate from that intelligible light
which descends upon the Ideas, which was the opinion
of the Phoenician philosophers and was afterwards
accepted by the Platonists Iamblichus[5] and Julian[6].
On that account the Poet speaks of the first, the
heavenly Venus, who continuously looks at herself in
the divine sun, and says in the sun to show that the
Mind, turning to God with all its strength, is united

92

to Him as intimately as possible. He says that <u>in
its light half-furled the first is wont to
contemplate her face</u>, that is, in the shade of the
essence of the Angelic Mind which, making that ideal
light somewhat dim and faint by its weakness, is said
by the Poet to make a shade for itself. And he says
that this essence of the Mind is accustomed to
contemplate itself in this Venus, because by those
Ideas the former, as we have said elsewhere, becomes
intellectual.

This he says thus: <u>as from the radiance it sheds
on her</u> she takes all her riches, that is, of the
divine splendor, so she'll <u>confer</u>, give, communicate,
and share her light with <u>the last</u>, with sensible
beauty, from which the vulgar love is born in the
same way as the heavenly love from that other. Just
as the vulgar always woos, follows, and desires the
former, so also the heavenly does the latter, as was
said above, and therefore he finishes by saying:

> . . . As heavenly love has sat
> With her, just so the vulgar follows that.

[1] 42d/
[2] Reading <u>potesse</u> for <u>potessi</u>.
[3] <u>Genesis</u> 1:3.
[4] <u>Psalms</u> 36:9.
[5] Syrian Neo-Platonist, c. 250-330.
[6] The Roman emperor Julian the apostate, c. 331-363, who attempted to return the empire to paganism in a more or less Neo-Platonic form.
[7] Benivieni uses the masculine pronoun here.

Sixth Stanza

<u>When first formed</u>. . . .

Before getting into the exposition of this
stanza, in which is shown how the particular beauty
of one body kindles the fire of love in the mind of
another, it will be nothing if not advantageous to
throw some light of knowledge on that aforesaid
beauty. It is therefore to be considered that in the
beauty of bodies, which manifests itself to us by the
light of day, two things appear to whoever considers

them well. The first is the material arrangement of
the body, which consists in the right quantity of its
parts and in their suitable quality. The quality is
a matter of their shape and color. The second thing
is a certain quality which cannot be called by a more
appropriate name than grace, which appears and shines
in beautiful things, and it seems to me that it
properly claims for itself the name of Venus, or
beauty, because it is this alone which lights the
fire of love in human hearts. Many would have it
that this results and is born from the basic
composition of the body, that from the arrangement,
shape, and hues of its limbs, taken as a whole, this
grace results. Against this opinion, in my judgment,
experience should be enough, because many times we
shall see a body not deficient from any angle and
perfect in every part in regard to the above
conditions but nevertheless lacking every grace, and
in contrast there will nevertheless sometimes be seen
a wonderful grace in a body which could well enough
be better proportioned[1] Catullus puts this very well
in one of his epigrams[1], where he says:

> Beautiful to many Quintia seems.
> My eyes confess her fair and tall and straight,
> Each part of her itself a thing for dreams,
> But I deny that taken as a whole they rate
> So high, for on so big a stalk false blooms
> Don't shine with any grace to venerate.

The poet concedes to Quintia the quality of
complexion in her fairness and that of shape in her
straightness and also the quantity which is sought in
the beautiful, which is height. Nevertheless in no
way does he concede that he can call her beautiful,
because she lacks that <u>Venus</u> and grace which, we
said, is to physical beauty as salt to any dish.

What, therefore, shall we say is the reason why
one body is endowed with such grace and another lacks
it? I shall say what I think it is, submitting my
judgment to any better opinion. I believe that since
such an effect does not come from the body it
necessarily has to be attributed to the quality of
the soul, which, I believe, when it is very perfect
and luminous in itself, transfuses some ray of its
own splendor even into the earthly body. All the
ancient philosophers and theologians agree on this.
When Moses descended from the mountain and the vision

of God, his face was so lustrous that the eyes of the
people could not bear it, and he spoke to them with
his face veiled.[2] Porphyry writes that every time
the soul of Plotinus was exalted in some sublime
contemplation a wonderful splendor appeared in his
face.[3] And this is what Plotinus writes, that no one
beautiful was ever bad. Plotinus will have it that
this beauty, this grace, which often appears in a
body not even moderately beautiful in either stature
or complexion, is a very sure sign of the intrinsic
perfection of the soul.[4] It is in speaking of this
perfection that Solomon says in Proverbs: "The wisdom
of a man maketh his face to shine."[5] I believe this
opinion is fully verified in the three observed
characteristics of the holy name of the primordial
Adam[6], and whoso can understand this secret, let him
understand. A Platonist would add that the souls
which descend from the sphere of Venus should above
all others have such an effect on their bodies.

[1]86. I have translated Pico's Italian version
of Catullus here rather than the original Latin, from
which it differs somewhat in meaning.
[2]Exodus 34:29.
[3]Vita Plotini XIII.
[4]Enneads I, vi, 6.
[5]Pico seems to have trusted his memory on this
quotation. It is actually Ecclesiastes 8:1.
[6]Cf. II Enoch 30:13-15.

SIXTH, SEVENTH, AND EIGHTH STANZAS

When first formed. . . .

It is the order of the universe that from
separate and intelligible things proceed the lesser
ones, and the latter, turning back towards their
causes, return to them so far as they can. I see
this wonderfully indicated in the present poem where
our Poet, having to treat of love and beauty, first
began with the heavenly beauty and the heavenly love
and said enough of their nature, origin, and
particular qualities in the third and fourth stanzas.
Then in the fifth stanza he told how from these came
physical beauty and the love for it. Now in the rest
of the poem the author shows us how from sensible

beauty one rises by regular steps to intelligible beauty, having arrived at which he ends his work, since on reaching that, every amorous desire should come to an end.

Whoever has to treat of such things can follow no more subtle, systematic, nor adequate method than our Poet has here learnedly pursued. A method known and understood by only a few, it is what Plato in the _Philebus_ calls deriving the many from the one and the one from the many. Whoever knows how to do this properly, Plato writes, we ought to follow like a god, a person truly divine, an earthly angel, fit to go up and down the ladder of Jacob as he wishes in company with the other contemplative angels.

We shall discuss this series of steps at length in our commentary on the _Symposium_. Following our present author, however, this order shows how by six steps, starting with material beauty, man is led to his final goal. If to the soul focused on the senses there is first presented by the eyes the particular beauty of Alcibiades or Phaedrus or some other outwardly pleasing body, it inclines towards that and delights itself in that particular form, and stopping here on the first step it is most imperfect and material. The Poet assigns the reason for this effect at the beginning of this stanza, that is, he tells how it happens that one feels affection for one person more quickly than for another.

The second step is taken when the soul refashions in itself the image received by the eyes with its inner, but still material and fanciful, powers and makes it as much more perfect as it makes it more spiritual, and separating it more from matter makes it approach the ideal beauty, although still very remote from it.

The third step is taken when by the light of the Active Intellect the soul, separating the form it has perceived from every particularity considers the true nature of physical beauty and no longer pays attention to the particular image of a single body but to the universal beauty of all bodies taken together. This is the last step reached by the soul dominated by the senses. Although at this step it looks at beauty in itself and not as restricted to the bosom of any material object, nevertheless it

96

receives such knowledge from particular sensations and particular fancies, from which it comes about that whoever arrives at a knowledge of the nature of things in this way alone cannot see them plainly and without a veil of the greatest ambiguity. Many Peripatetics, especially Latin ones, have believed and do believe that our souls cannot rise to perfect knowledge while united to our bodies, a view which we shall demonstrate in our debate to be very alien to the thought of Aristotle and of almost all of the Arab and Greek Peripatetics.

The fourth step is that the soul, reflecting on its operations, sees that it recognizes the nature of beauty universally, not as limited to any particular thing, and it realizes that everything which is founded upon matter is particular, from which it concludes that such universality as this comes not from the sensible external object but from its own inner light and power. Therefore it says to itself: "If this beauty appears to me in the dim mirrors of natural appearances only by the strength of my own light, surely it is reasonable that by looking into the mirror of my own substance, free from cloud and shadow, every such thing ought to be seen more clearly." Concentrating thus on itself it sees the image of the ideal beauty participated in by the Intellect, as was said in the second book. This is the fourth step, the perfect image of heavenly love, as was said above.

Ascending then from here to its own proper Intellect is the fifth step, in which the heavenly Venus shows herself to the soul in her true guise and not an imaginary one, though not in the complete plenitude of her beauty, for which in an individual intellect there is no room. Eager and thirsty for this, the soul tries to unite its individual and particular intellect with the primal and universal one, the first created thing, the ultimate and universal dwelling of ideal beauty.

Reaching this, the sixth step in the sequence, the soul ends its journey, and it is not allowed to move on to the seventh, the sabbath, as it were, of heavenly love. Here it should rest happily in its goal, at the side of the First Father, the fountain of beauty.

These are the steps of the ladder of love by
which one ascends to the true, complete, and distinct
knowledge of this topic of love. These steps, and
how one makes the ascent from one to another, I do
not know if in the sixth, seventh, and eighth stanzas
the Poet describes with more gracefulness of verse or
profundity of doctrine. Before he passes on to that,
however, at the beginning of the sixth stanza he
gives the reason why one is drawn more to the love of
this one than of that one. This reason, although it
is based on all the principles of the Platonists, I
nevertheless do not remember ever having read
elsewhere.

To understand it one must first know that among
human souls the Platonists say that some are like
Saturn, some like Jupiter, and so on with the other
planets, and by this they mean that one soul will
have a closer kinship and conformity to the soul of
the heaven of Saturn than to the soul of the heaven
of Jupiter, and another the opposite. This is for no
other reason than that one soul is of this nature and
another one of that, and there is no other intrinsic
cause to be assigned for this, for which the
extrinsic, and efficient, cause is that which
produces these souls, the artificer of the world of
which Plato speaks in the Timaeus, who, scattering
the seed, sows some souls in the moon, and others in
the planets and stars, which he calls the instruments
of time.[2]

In the second place it should be known that
since the soul immediately unites itself with its
heavenly vehicle, as was also said in the first book
to be the opinion of the Platonists, and by means of
that to the earthly and corruptible body, some, whose
belief follows our author's on this, will have it
that the rational soul descending from its star does
itself form the earthly body which it has to govern.

Starting from these principles, the Poet
imagines that into the vehicle of the descending
soul, which is enlivened with that power with which
it forms the earthly body, there is infused by its
star a formative virtue for the corruptible body, and
according to what comes down from one star or another
souls receive the formative virtue differently.
Because of this, the physiognomists speak of one man
as having a lunar face, another a solar face, another

98

a mercurial one, another a saturnine, another a martial, and from the countenance they judge the soul to be of like nature. But because the lower matter is not always obedient to that which shapes and stamps it, the power of the soul cannot always express in the earthly body the appearance it would like, from which it comes about that there can be two jovial persons who appear dissimilar in form, because at the conception of one the matter will have been differently disposed to receive that kind of soul rather than another. What is perfect in one is in the other always like something unbegun and not absolute.

Our Poet therefore wishes it to be the appearance of two bodies, shaped by the power of the same star, which generates between them the harmonious adjustment and agreement of intense love. Therefore the Poet says <u>that when first formed by the face of God</u>, the soul[3], whether immediately, as the Catholics will have it, or mediately, according to the Platonists, "<u>departs in order to descend down here . . . to enter into human hearts</u>." Because the heart is a more appropriate abode for the soul, which by its nature is the source of life and warmth, and by its continuous motion is a symbol of the heavens, from which it comes, much is in agreement.

. . . from that exalted sphere,
Where dwells the Sun. . . .

that is, from Cancer, raised highest of all the twelve signs of the Zodiac above this highest heaven of ours, and this is the opinion of the Platonists, who say that the soul descends from Cancer and rises from Capricorn. I believe that their basis for this may be that Cancer is the house of the moon, whose power rules especially over the animating, vegetative part of bodies, and Capricorn is the house of Saturn, placed in authority over the contemplation for which the soul released from the body is free.

<u>There</u>, that is, in earthly human bodies, the soul <u>manifesting with amazing arts</u>, arts surely divine and wonderful because of the Father's wish for the intellectual wisdom and reason of the soul to be infused into its heavenly nature. <u>That worth</u> is that formative virtue of the elemental body, the worth <u>she brought from stars that rule her role and which,</u>

99

compacted[4] whole, remains among her spoil[5] from heaven's marts --that is, her heavenly vehicle in which she lives and incloses herself. Therefore expressing the figure in such power, in human seed as best she bears its smarts she makes her lodging[6], the soul's inn, this sensible organic body in which the soul takes up her lodging in this world. But that human seed is more or less resistant to heavenly care, as we said above.

Whenever from the Sun -- from the splendor of the beauty -- that's graven there -- in the body molded by such a soul -- there comes into another's heart the imprint of the figure imprinted on it. He means that every time such a face is seen by someone else, some seemly soul -- if it is a face produced by a star in conformity with the star of him who looks at it -- then blazes up its lamp with the fire of that sort of love. And this, as I have said, is the first step.

The soul which bears it: here are indistinctly contained the second and third steps. It is to be noted that at the end of the sixth stanza and in the beginning of the seventh the Poet summarizes and touches generally on the ascent from the first step to the last, pointing out their differences but not elaborating on them, following in this the order established by the philosophers, especially by the Peripatetics in the preface to Aristotle's Physics, where the confused and indistinct knowledge of a thing precedes the clear explanation of it.[7] This our Poet has observed here, who, having already thrown some light on this step in an implicit compendium now makes clear in the phrase in three shining mirrors that which he promised in touching upon it briefly in the preceding verses. Not without mystery does our Poet join these three stanzas so that the meaning of the end of the sixth stanza is furnished in the beginning of the seventh, and of the end of this in the beginning of the eighth. To any who do not consider further, this would perhaps seem contrary to the scheme of the poem as a whole, in which it seems proper for every stanza to be furnished with its own explanation, as provided by the Poet in the first five and the last. But he has chosen to show by this arrangement here that one should stop on no step before the last, nor propose

100

it as an end to his love, but use each step always as a ladder to the next.

It is not praiseworthy to delight in the figure of a handsome youth unless you use it as a means to looking within yourself at the proportion and fitting quality of that figure even apart from that gross and material body in which you have seen it. To ocupy the imagination in considering the figure of one body cannot be other than a vain activity if you stop at that and do not use it as a means for contemplating with your reason the beauty which is universal in all bodies. The soul cannot be other than weak and infirm which, always prostrate above the body, never straightens up and, betaking itself to itself, recognizes its own treasures but, as Asaph says, being placed in dignity and honor, does not know itself and becomes like the silly brutes which lack the power of self-awareness. In itself or by itself the soul will not be able to possess enough of that light of beauty, which it does not have from itself but only as a gift or communication from others, if it does not return to Him who made it a particpant in that particular river. If it wishes to satisfy its thirst completely, it must take itself to the primal sea of beauty immediately emanating from that fountain, thus imitating our Poet who, beginning in the sixth stanza to display the steps of this stairway by which one ascends from earth to heaven, does not stop with his verses until he has reached the Highest Good.

By which in love are formed and beautified
The mind, the soul, the world, and what's
    allied.

For this reason there are really only seven stanzas, although the poem is divided into nine, because none of these three supplies its own explanation, though one results for all of them together. Therefore, with the sixth stanza completed, the Poet stops, like every lover on the sixth step, and just starting to go beyond, he feels love gathering up the reins, showing us by this that no one who reaches the sixth step is permitted to proceed further, because that is the end of the road of love, although one may go beyond it by way of another love, the love with which God loves Himself as Himself rather than as the creator of ideal

101

beauty, but this is not the love of which we are speaking, because this is not a desire for beauty, which, according to the Platonists, is not found in God because of His infinite simplicity, as we said in the first book. Now, returning to the exposition of the text, the Poet says, combining the second and third steps, that then <u>the soul which bears</u> the image received by the eyes imagines and <u>brightens</u> it <u>with its rays and feigns</u>[8], <u>the more to praise, the mark more fair</u> -- with the rays, that is, of its imaginative, or truly thinking faculty, and of its rational one.

<u>And thus</u>: he shows that from his statement it can be understood why sometimes, or almost always, the beloved seems a great deal more handsome to the lover than he really is, because the lover looks not at the beloved but at the image which his soul has made of him, and the more he has separated it from its matter, the source of every deformity, the more beautiful he has made it. Moreover, the figure which the soul has formed in itself seems more beautiful than the external appearance because it is in truth more beautiful, even if one admits that, being made and generated by the soul, the soul takes more delight in it as a thing of its own than it would take in the thing itself. And therefore the Poet adds:

> The heart on sweet delusion feeds, and views
> Its cherished inner object as its
>   child . . .

that is, as its own work and creation, made and generated by it.

> Sometimes re-styled . . . .

Here the author shows how from the fourth step one reaches the ultimate end, omitting explicit statement of the means, the fifth and sixth steps, by which one reaches it, but which he indicates when he says <u>from step to step</u>. He says, therefore, that sometimes the soul forms that universal image anew <u>beneath the holy light's resplendent streams</u>, the light of the ideal beauty shared by it. This is the <u>rare and heavenly gift</u>, because few receive it, only those who are very perfect and who are so few that, as I said above, many judge it to be impossible for

man to reach this step. On this account he says <u>rare</u>
<u>and heavenly gift</u>.

   <u>By mild ascent</u>, with the re-styling done, which
is the fourth step, <u>from step to step</u>, from the fifth
step, which is its own particular intellect, the soul
rises to the sixth step of union with the primal and
universal Intellect, <u>that birthless sun</u>, God, by
Whom, although through many intermediaries, as he
immediately adds, is formed that light of beauty
which appears in the beloved body because "one sun",
a single light which emanates from the divine visage,
reflected, as it were, from three mirrors, the
Angelic Mind, the spirit or rational nature, and the
body or sensible world, so adorns it.

   <u>From here</u>: here the Poet duly explains the
aforesaid steps, of which we said enough at the
beginning of the interpretation of the sixth stanza.
He says, therefore, starting from the first and
lowest step, that <u>from here</u>, from the body, <u>the showy</u>
<u>spoils are seized by eyes</u>, the spoils of the sort of
beauty found in the body, which, as I said above, is
the first step and the most material. Then he adds
<u>the other handmaid who there has her place</u>, where he
declares how the appearance of the object passes from
the visual faculty of the eyes, which is an outer
sense, to the imaginative faculty, which is an inner
sense. The imaginative faculty he calls <u>the other</u>
<u>handmaid</u>[9] <u>of the</u>[10] <u>heart</u>, by the heart meaning the
substance of the rational soul, which both the inner
and outer sensitive powers serve and minister to, as
all the philosophers agree. Those spoils or outward
forms, being conceived by the imagination, the Poet
says that they are <u>sometimes taken to trace new</u>
<u>traits</u> not shown by it, because the imagination, like
a higher and more noble faculty of sensation, also
makes those appearances more spiritual by plucking
them further from the imperfection of their matter,
which does not receive into itself the form of the
true Venus, although being still a material and
organic potentiality, it cannot reduce those
appearances to perfect immateriality.

   For that reason he says that the imagination re-
traces the appearance but does not show it. This is
the second step, which, although it is love of a
particular body, nevertheless no longer loves that
particular beauty in that gross and fleshly personage

103

but in the image which the lover has formed of it in his soul. As this step is more perfect than the first, so also it is happier, because the lover derives no less enjoyment in the absence of the beloved than in his presence. He has the beloved always with him; he sees and hears and converses with him familiarly. Anyone on the first step is happy in so far as the beloved is present to him, a condition in every way much better than that bestial non-love and furor whose good can last only for a little while and cannot leave behind it anything but long-lasting bitterness and repentence. This ought to be sufficient incentive for anyone to make swift flight from this execrable sensual pleasure and to hasten on a speedy course to that heavenly love where no trace of misery, but every abundance of happiness, is to be found.

It ought not to allure anyone to this wretched sensuality that many men famous for their sanctity and prudence and learning have been caught up in it. Rather, this fact ought to serve as a most efficacious warning to everyone that it should be avoided with all one's ingenuity. If this evil is so poisonous and pernicious that it has been able to generate almost incurable weaknesses in such strong and perfect souls, everyone should without doubt be persuaded that in his own it may give birth to a deadly disease fatal to all. One can properly conclude from this that whoever crashes over such a precipice deserves not only correction and fatherly punishment from God for himself and his badly-composed thoughts but from man perhaps no less pity and compassion than blame.

Returning now to the words of the Poet, since he has spoken of the first and second steps, he says coming to the third: the many varied charms. . . . It is here that the soul, rising above the first and second steps, on neither of which beauty particularly divests itself of matter, considers that quality as a universal concept, and within itself reduces the multitude of particular beautiful bodies to a unity of beauty. This is properly the beauty of what rises aloft from down here below, of what reduces the multitude into its own unity, as was said above.

Thus Love with this delights. . . . In this universal knowledge the soul takes delight as in something fabricated by itself, as we also said a little above, and it sees in it the light of true beauty, though only as sunlight is seen under water. The source of the light is in the sky, and from there it comes to the water through the two intervening mediums of fire and air. Likewise from God, the first and intelligible source of the light of beauty, through the two intermediate grades of the intellectual ideal and of the reason shared by the soul, just as through fire and air, the light of true beauty shines in the universal Form abstracted from the senses, as in water.

Some flashes from the god. . . . This is the ascent from the third step to the fourth, to the Ideas in which the soul participates, in which no longer the shadow of beauty but true beauty is seen, although only the participated rather than the essential.

Thus once the heart, of which he declares: _Within its mind that glory will appear._ Then he adds: _To light more sharp and clear._ This is the ascent from the fifth step to the sixth, in which one's own particular intellect unites with the first and universal Mind, a great deal more open and clear than ours, the Mind which is immediately next to God, the first and intelligible sun. On that account he says _it flies suspended near that orb_, by whose living light the mind, the soul, and the world are made beautiful, as we have stated at length above.

[1] 16c ff.
[2] 42d.
[3] Here, as in other quotations from Benivieni, Pico varies the poet's word order slightly.
[4] Pico has _raccolto_ here rather than Benivieni's _accolto_, though the meanings are similar.
[5] This word is plural in the poem.
[6] Pico's word _luce_ here, "light", I take to be an erroneous transcription of Benivieni's word _lime_, which I have translated "smarts" and which seems to make better sense.
[7] I, 1, 189a, 22.
[8] Pico supplies here the verb _effinge_ in place of Benivieni's _effige_, which seems a misprint.

105

Ministra, vs. ancilla in the poem.
10 For Benivieni's definite article el Pico
substitutes the possessive del, making the
imaginative faculty the handmaid of the heart, but by
a possible interpretation de-emphasizing the sense-
imagination-heart sequence.

Final Stanza

My song, I feel Love gathering up the reins. . .

It was the opinion of the ancient theologians
that divine and secret mysteries ought not rashly to
be made public except so far as permitted from above.
Therefore the Poet pretends, as if ready to say more,
to be restrained by Love and commanded by him to show
common people only the outer bark of the mysteries of
love, keeping the pith of the true sense only for
more elevated and perfect intellects, a rule observed
by all of the ancients who have written holy things.
Origen writes that Jesus Christ revealed many
mysteries to his disciples which they did not choose
to write down but communicated only by mouth to
whoever seemed worthy of them. Dionysius the
Areopagite confirms having observed this among our
priests, who received from each other in succession
an understanding of the secrets which it was not
permissible to put into writing. Expounding to
Timothy some of the names of God and the many
profound meanings of the angelic and ecclesiastical
hierarchies, Dionysius commands him to keep the book
hidden and not reveal it except to the few who may be
worthy of such knowledge.

This procedure was observed most scrupulously
among the ancient Hebrews, and their science of this,
in which is contained the exposition of the abstruse
and recondite mysteries of the law, is called Cabala,
which means reception, because one received it from
another not in writing but orally, in succession.
This is a science truly divine and worthy of not
being shared except with a few, a major foundation of
our faith, desire for which alone moved me to the
assiduous study of the Hebrew and Chaldean languages,
without which it is completely impossible to come to
a knowledge of it. The extent to which the same

procedure was practiced by the Pythagoreans is seen in the letter of Lysis[1] to Hipparchus, and for no other reason did the Egyptians have sphinxes carved in all their temples except that divine things, when they are written down, ought to be covered with enigmatic veils and poetic dissimulation, as to the best of our ability we have shown our Poet to have done in the present poem and as we shall show to have been done by the other Greek and Latin poets in our treatise on poetic theology.

[1]Philosopher of Tarentum, fl. c. 400 B.C.

SELECTED BIBLIOGRAPHY

Barone, Giuseppe, Giovanni Pico della Mirandola,
    Milan, 1948.
Cassirer, E., Kristeller, P. O., & Randall, Jr.,
    J. H., eds., The Renaissance Philosophy of
    Man, Chicago, University of Chicago, 1948.
Convegno di studi pichiani, Studi Pichiani,
    Modena, Aedes Muratoriana, 1965.
Cordier, Pierre M. Jean Pic de la Mirandole,
    Paris, Debresse, 1957.
Encyclopedia of Philosophy, ed. Paul Edwards,
    New York, Macmillan, 1967.
Kristeller, Paul O., Renaissance Thought, New
    York, Harper, 1961.
More, Sir Thomas, Giovanni Pico della Mirandola,
    His Life by His Nephew, ed. J. M. Rigg,
    London, Nutt, 1890.
Napoli, Giovanni di, Giovanni Pico della Mirandola
    a la problematica dottrina del suo tempo, Roma,
    Desclee, 1965.
Nelson, John C., Renaissance Theory of Love, New
    York, Columbia, 1958.
Pater, Walter, Studies in the History of the
    Renaissance, London, Macmillan, 1873.
Pico della Mirandola, Giovanni, De Hominis
    Dignitate, Heptaplus, De Ente et Uno, ed.
    Eugenio Garin, Firenze, Vallechi, 1942.
-----, Heptaplus, tr. Jessie B. McGaw, New York,
    Philosophical Library, 1977.
-----, Of Being and Unity, tr. Victor M. Hamm,
    Milwaukee, Marquette, 1943.
-----, On the Dignity of Man (tr. Charles Glenn
    Wallis), On Being and the One, (tr. Paul J. W.
    Miller), Heptaplus (tr. Douglas Carmichael),
    Indianapolis, Bobbs-Merrill, 1965.
-----, A Platonick Discourse Upon Love, tr. Thomas
    Stanley, ed. Edmund G. Gardner, Boston,
    Merrymount, 1914.
Plato, Dialogues, tr. Jowett, New York, Random House,
    1937.
Symonds, John Addington, Renaissance in Italy,
    London, Smith & Elder, 1877.
Vignal, L. Gautier, Pic de la Mirandole, Paris,
    Grasset, 1937.

ABOUT THE TRANSLATOR

Douglas Carmichael was born in Greenwich, Connecticut, and is a graduate of Bowdoin College, with an M.A. in English from Harvard and a Ph.D. from Indiana University. Since 1958 he has been on the faculty of St. Lawrence University, serving for nineteen years as chairman of the philosophy department. During World War II he served as an Intalian interpreter in the U.S. Army. His translation of Pico della Mirandola's Heptaplus (Bobbs-Merrill) was published in 1965. He is also the author of Pendragon, an historical novel about the rise of King Arthur.